THE
CRAFT
ADVANTAGE

THE CRAFT ADVANTAGE

Reviving Craft in Architecture for a Better Built Environment and Improved Influence

BY BEAU DROMIACK

Copyright © 2023 by Beau Dromiack. All rights reserved.

Published by Press 49, a division of BMH Companies, Chandler, Arizona

No part of this publication may be reproduced, stored in a retrieval system, or transmitted in any form or by any means, electronic, mechanical, photocopying, recording, scanning, or otherwise without the prior written permission of the Publisher. Requests to the Publisher for permissions should be addressed to the Permissions Department, Press 49, 4980 S. Alma School Road, Ste 2-493, Chandler, AZ 85248, 202.630.1218, or online at www.press49.com/permissions

Limit of Liability/Disclaimer of Warranty: While the publisher and author have used their best efforts in preparing this book, they make no representations or warranties with respect to the accuracy or completeness of the contents of this book and specifically disclaim any implied warranties of merchantability or fitness for a particular purpose. No warranty may be created or extended by sales representatives or written sales materials. The advice contained herein may not be suitable for your situation. Neither the publisher nor the author shall be liable for any loss of profit or any other commercial damages, including but not limited to, special, incidental, consequential, or other damages.

The views expressed in this publication are those of the author; are the responsibility of the author; and do not necessarily reflect or represent the views of Press 49, its parent company, its owner, or its partners.

Volume pricing is available to bulk orders placed by corporations, associations, and others. For bulk order details and for media inquiries, please contact Press 49 at info@press49.com or 833.PRESS49 (833.773.7749).

FIRST EDITION

Library of Congress Control Number: 2023913671
ISBN: 978-1-953315-31-1 (paperback)
ISBN: 978-1-953315-33-5 (eBook)

ARC000000: ARCHITECTURE / General
ARC015000: ARCHITECTURE / Professional Practice

Book design by Artichoked Creative
Photographs, diagrams, and content created by Beau Dromiack

Printed in the United States of America

DEDICATION

This book is dedicated to my glorious wife, Tab, who has endured many years of tolerating intense conversation about the future of architecture, among other often annoying topics that interest me.

This book is also dedicated to the many people I have had the opportunity to work with in my pursuit of knowledge, wisdom, and experience in our profession of architecture. This knowledge will be further transferred in future publications about our profession.

"There are many professionals out there, but only a few are truly architects."

LOUIS I. KAHN

FOREWORD

I have known Beau for 25 years. Beau has infectious enthusiasm and energy toward life, music, backpacking, invention, and architecture. We are friends that have shared the adventure of learning together and, separately, our very complex profession—the good, the bad, and, as Beau would say, "the glorious." We both excelled and loved the macro and micro aspects of our craft; he focused on the macro drivers impacting our profession, while I focused on developing my art and story of detail and craft. It was he who planted the idea in my mind to work at the Morphosis architecture firm, which I did and learned from. Whenever we saw each other, Beau's increasing knowledge and pursuit of our profession in practice inspired and motivated me to see the macro trends that impact all of us who have a passion for excellence for a meaningful built environment. I find the mission of his book to be for all of us who want to acknowledge and reverse the downward trends in our profession and find the balance of sustainable growth, passion, and effectiveness.

It takes a fine balance that demands patience and equanimity between logos and pathos to create an ethos in art and architecture. Architecture is a search, a relentless pursuit of the sublime through the churning of thoughts that ultimately assume a form that is a wrapper of space within space. It is iterative in nature through constant testing, rejecting, and accepting that ultimately land the architect at the sweet-spot solution. The ideal pursuit of an architect is to strive to give back and practice and improve our skill in the many aspects of our craft to maximize the potential for each opportunity. The artist inside, though, is never fulfilled and remains thirsty to improve and grow. My favorite contemporary architect, Glenn

Murcutt, says, "Life is not about maximizing everything; it's about giving something back—like light, space, form, serenity, joy. You have to give something back."

Until the Renaissance period, more formal construction documents and drawings were not a part of the creative process. The profession was widely regarded as a "craft," along with sculpture and painting—something to be created, evolved, and tested at the construction site. Architecture as the art form and craft has been endangered between shrewd profit-making and the trends of superficial novelty arising and passing. If one is truly committed and serious, the profession is very noble and adds profound value to the built environment. The immense long-term satisfaction one gets through meaningful craft can outweigh the monetary gains. Profits in good hands could get reinvested and potentially facilitate creating and refining in even more meaningful ways. An architect can maximize impact by taking the time to hear the client's needs, then embarking on a journey to craft with care and a solution that resonates and transcends function. "Care" is the foundation of the craft and sustainable practices . . . It is not an exercise in theory alone but also in crafting within reality by collaborating with the craftsperson in the field to inspire and achieve the best quality.

The Finnish architect and author Juhani Pallasmaa presents this concept very well in *The Thinking Hand: Existential and Embodied Wisdom in Architecture*: "Alvar Alto was a master in his communication with the various professionals and craftsmen of his varied productions; the highly respected academician spoke to a carpenter and bricklayer as his equals and inspired them to internalize their work and perform supremely at the limit of their professional abilities. Mastering one craft personally helps the designer and architect to grasp the nuances of other crafts and, before all, to respect the special skill and experience of the craftsman executing his design. Besides, learning any skill intimately teaches one welcome humility. Arrogance does not go with true skill."

The Italian architect Renzo Piano further illustrates the point: "You start by sketching, then you do drawings, then you make a model, and then you go to reality—you go to the site—and then you go back to the drawing. You build up a kind of circularity between drawings and making and back again."

Simply put, architecture is the craft of hand, mind, and action. The profession is facing profound challenges at a multitude of levels, including, but not limited to, the transactional education system, students teaching students, eroded mentorship and craftsmanship, lack of noble commitment toward the practice, consumerist and disposable culture, visual noise of social media, and so on. With the many challenges that lie before the profession of architecture, I feel that Beau Dromiack's *The Craft Advantage* is a crucial clarion call to our profession for how we need to reconsider our actions, mind our past, and grow our profession into the future to revive its true glory to serve humanity and the environment equally. Beau describes the challenge and provides the observations and tools to retool how we can move forward to revive craft as a core value in our profession.

Amit Upadhye, AIA
July 2023
Scottsdale, Arizona

"If you want to overcome the whole world, overcome yourself."

FYODOR DOSTOEVSKY

I AM A FAN OF REALITY.

The overarching purpose of this book is to draw attention to a decline as I see it: to revive craft as a core value, to reverse the decline, and to increase our influence as architects for a better built environment and profession.

CONTENTS

THE MISSION

Introduction	1
Author's Summary	5
The Big Idea	8
Craft by Definition	10
Where Craft Can Be Seen	12
24 Questions and AI	14
Three Components That Define the Craft Advantage	18
Opportunities and Possibilities	20
The Built Environment	25
Turn Up the Craft Dial	28

THE FRICTION

The Decline Trend and the Skeptical Architect	33
The Decline Sequence Toward Reduced Influence	40
The Decline Trend: Introduction	42
The Trend Diagrams	46
The Mechanics to Reverse the Decline and Grow Influence	60

THE SKILLS

Whole-Building Thinker (and the Power of Perforated Silos)	65
Intelligent Idea Integration (Growing Influence)	81
Accountability and Mentorship (Follow-Through and Growth)	97
Skills to Shape	111
Conclusion	179

THE MISSION

"Architecture is the learned game, correct and magnificent, of forms assembled in the light."

LE CORBUSIER

THE STRAW VIEW

THE MISSION

INTRODUCTION

Early in my career, I started to realize "like a splinter in [my] mind" (to quote Morpheus in *The Matrix*) that the context was getting lost in my singular focus of individual architecture expression. I was not seeing very well beyond my narrow view, or a *straw view* focus. The straw view is like looking through a straw and seeing only the perspective allowed by the narrow view within a straw. You see your target but without a wider gaze to see the context around and beyond it. When the object of the focus is complete, the straw view shifts to a new project focus but still without a wide gaze. It was during this time in my career that it occurred to me that the majority of architects are all looking through their own straws; some focus on profit, others focus on the next project to define a signature style, others focus on growing a business, and some are just trying to keep the doors open. Their actions are mostly driven by the straw view with a limited wider gaze. I believe this is one reason why the built environment never seems to improve and why our profession is in a slow decline.

Many of us are so busy with the straw view that we are not seeing the decline within our industry. We are not noticing, at any level of noticeable outrage, the impact that the decrease in craft is having holistically on our profession and the built environment. We

WIDENED GAZE

INTRODUCTION

are not noticing the resultant reduction of our influence, respect, and responsibilities from our industry partners. When we see something we don't like, we just shift the straw over to a beautiful building and ignore the less-inspiring and stressful context. The "we" is all of us as a profession, not the exceptions to the rule. Our tendency toward egocentricity helps us ignore the hard facts within the wider gaze—facts outside of the straw view.

It was these thoughts, churned over and over, that drove me to shift my trajectory from an interest in object or signature architecture to exploration to deepen my understanding of our profession and industry. My self-curated experiences have become the basis for this book. This attitude and shift may seem weird for a young architect at the time, but that is me in a nutshell. My passion shifted from the tree to the forest. Without the forest, the tree dies. Our profession is in decline. To save the trees, we need to maintain our forest. It is all interconnected.

I have worked within many different firm types, delivery models, and disciplines. I have experienced the artist/architect world, the cabinet and drafting shop, the massive engineering architecture world, and the construction and development world, and, throughout, I have experienced and developed expertise in a very broad range of building types, contractors, architects, clients, and integration complexities. I know now, for a fact, what I initially suspected many years earlier.

We need to embrace a new mission: share information, perforate silos, embrace integration, and reestablish and revive craft as our cultural imperative and core value. We need to drop the "straws" and widen our gaze to regain and increase our influence for a better built environment and an effective and lasting profession.

THE MISSION

AUTHOR'S SUMMARY

I have noticed three trends that have influenced me to write this book:

TREND 1: Architects have been losing influence through a reduction in craft excellence that, for so long, defined the core value of our profession. The profession has been in a slow decline over the last forty or more years due to a reduction in the quality of drawings, poor training, poor mentorship, underprepared graduates, siloed thinking and activity, and arrogance. These, combined with accelerated schedules and accelerated technology, have resulted in profit erosion and limited vision to make necessary intuitional changes to adapt to the accelerated curve that our industry and society, in general, have experienced and are currently experiencing. This trend of decline has created the coordination, quality, and craft vacuum that is starting to define our profession. The result is an increased risk to the builder and owner and the reduction of the influence of our profession. This reduction can result in losing our seat at the big table of decision-making. Why include someone that does not bring added value?

TREND 2: Contractors have filled the vacuum that architects have created. Their influence has increased, while architects' influence has decreased. When the quality of the design documents drops, the contractor is forced to fill any coordination gaps to reduce their own risk and prevent their own profit erosion. They have been doing this for many years, as seen by the addition to their construction services of the virtual design and construction teams, Revit, Bluebeam coordination, design coordination teams, and "architect replacement expertise." These actions have allowed the builer to manage risk, reduce risk, increase their influence with the owner, reduce profit erosion, and increase overall profit to continue to fill the void with even more effectiveness. The result of their increase in influence is the reduction of architects' influence in both perceived and practical needs that should be considered essential in the design process. The owner is realizing that their interests are more protected by the contractor than by the architect.

TREND 3: The overall design and building industry has been gravitating from design-bid-build delivery to Construction Manager at Risk, design-build, and integrated delivery platforms. Design-bid-build was the standard for many years, and, while it is still used today, the best value to the client is a platform that maximizes collaboration, reduces risk, and has an increased predictability of the outcome with clear accountability. Construction Manager at Risk and integrated delivery platforms provide these attributes, and where the most value to the client can be provided. It is this trend where architects have the best chance to retool and reverse the decline, increase influence, and maintain relevancy.

AUTHOR'S SUMMARY

Trends 1 and 2 are related by quality and risk. Trend 3 is an industry cultural trend fueled by a need to reduce risk and increase revenue by increasing the speed to market. An integrated delivery platform with a high-performing team is the quickest way to market and addresses both the private and public client's desire and need for the fewest variables and a more predictable outcome. Trend 3 is also the best opportunity for the architect to regain influence by pursuing the Craft Advantage and increasing beautiful design and a better built environment over time.

There are two overarching goals that are presented:

GOAL 1: Each professional, regardless of level and focus, should turn up the craft dial just a little in three categories, as described later in this book: (1) whole-building thinking, (2) intelligent idea integration, and (3) accountability and mentorship. Our built environment is not defined by the exceptions of the design excellence of the few but by the inertia of the mass of all the design decisions, good and bad.

GOAL 2: Clients, contractors, and the public see architecture as an essential need, not as a luxury. The goal is for the architect to be seen as the most essential resource for a joyous life experience in a better built environment. When this happens, we will have reversed the decline into a lasting and impactful existence, and we will have regained our influence beyond that of the contractor. The public will grow to expect that the skill and vision of an architect are essential for a better world.

The book is organized into three sections: the Mission to increase influence, the Friction that is defining the mission, and the Skills to shape the mission into a successful outcome.

THE **BIG** IDEA

THE BIG IDEA

Widen our gaze toward craft excellence as a revived core value and not a shifting priority.

Priorities change, but values are constant.

Craft is essential to reverse the decline and increase the architect's influence for a better built environment and an effective profession.

CRAFT BY DEFINITION

1 OXFORD DEFINITION

NOUN
An activity involving skill in making things by hand

VERB
Exercise skill in making (something)

2 COMMON INDUSTRY REFERENCE

Craft is typically in reference to the quality of drawings and the quality of construction.

3 MY DEFINITION OF THE CRAFT ADVANTAGE

"Craft is the integration of whole-building thinking, intelligent idea integration, and accountability into excellent delivery of quality, design, and relationships"

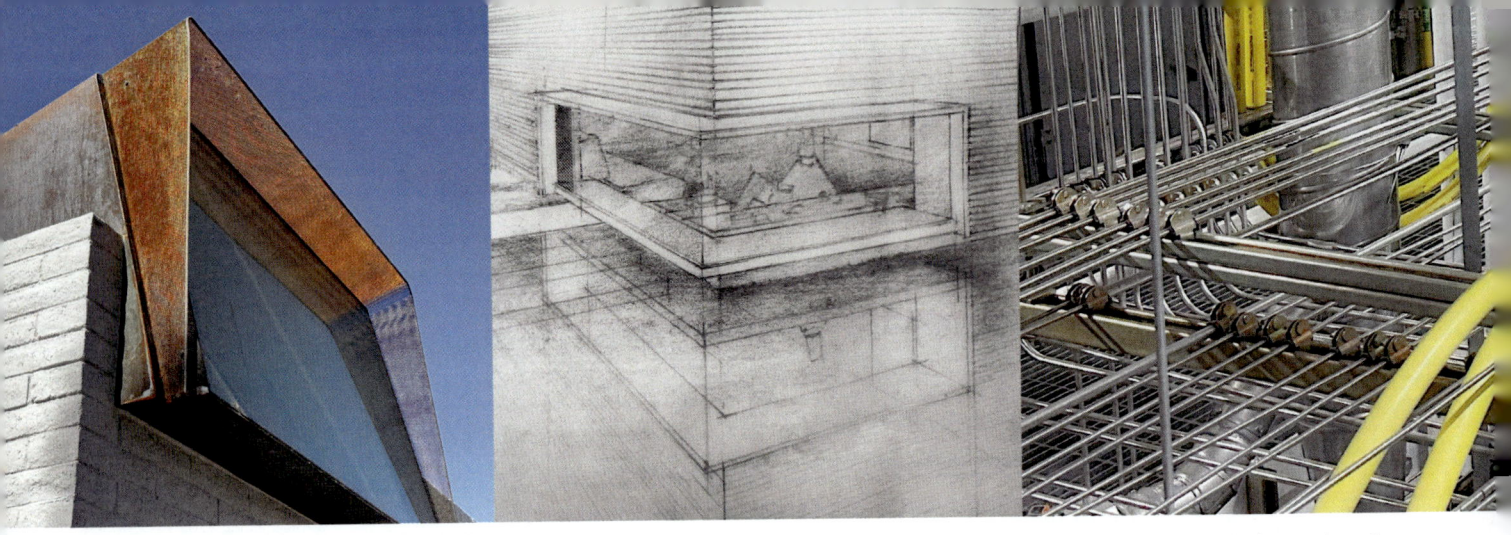

Details crafted with a story: the Polaris Skylight by Amit Upadhye

The craft of hand sketching

The craft of system design engineering

Craft can be seen in many places and activities.

Handcrafted construction details

The craft of creating learning tools

The craft of creating glorious ingredients

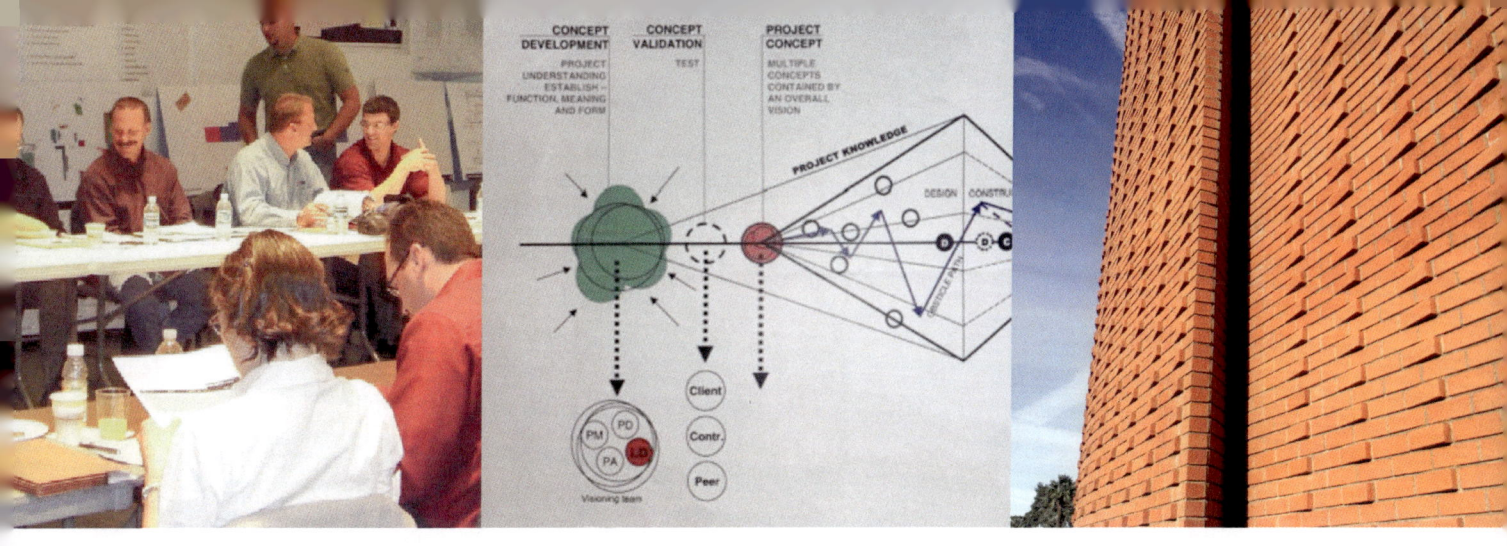

The craft of participating in meetings

The craft of creating diagrams

Construction crafted with care

Craft depends on a person's care to achieve quality.

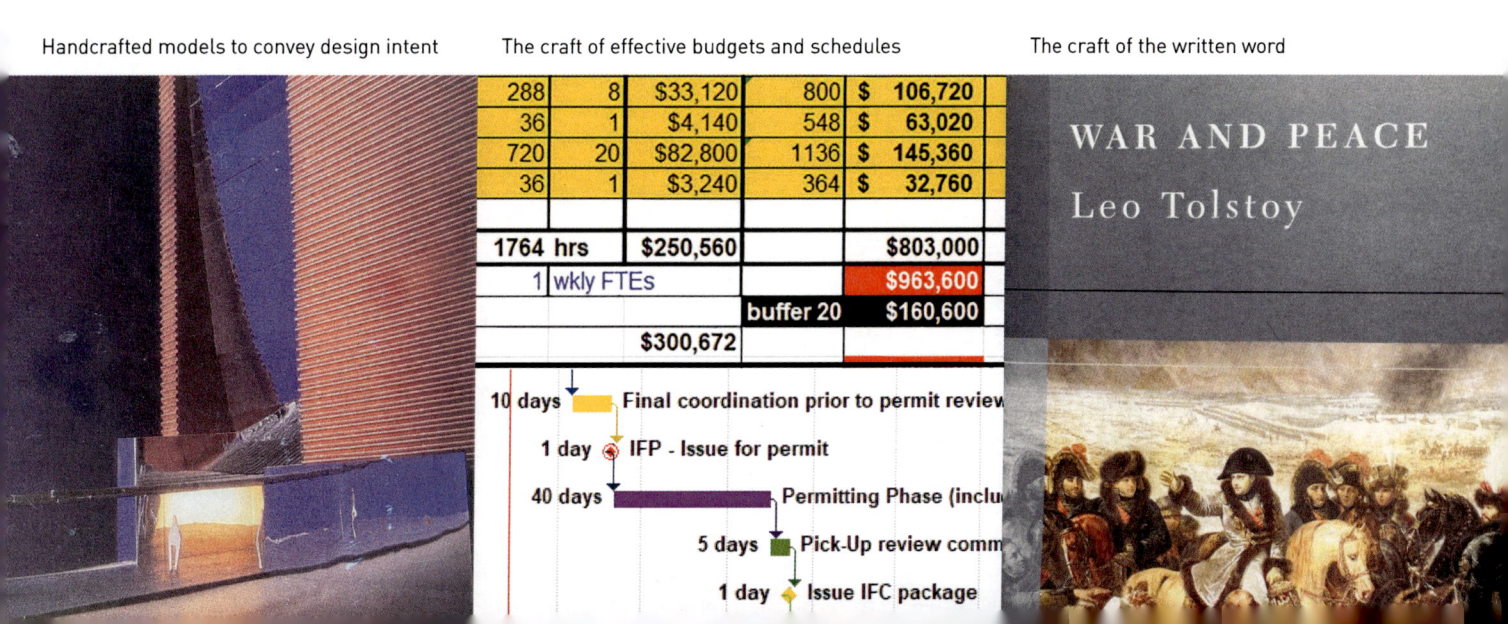

Handcrafted models to convey design intent

The craft of effective budgets and schedules

The craft of the written word

24 QUESTIONS

about Your Influence in Our Industry

AUTHOR'S SUMMARY

1. Are you invited to participate in the predesign development phase of a project?

2. Are you included in value engineering strategy meetings?

3. Are you asked to advise on your recommended design change?

4. Are you included by the contractor when a detail design change in the field is required?

5. Does the owner go to the contractor before going to you for design and coordination guidance?

6. Does the contractor include your team in pull-planning schedule sessions?

7. Is your advice requested for solving challenges in the field?

8. Do you trust that, during a page turn with the contractor and owner, the quality of your drawings will not embarrass you?

9. When confronted with a design question that a detail in the document set would address, are you confident that the detail is in the set?

10. Does the owner ask you to help select a site?

11. Does the owner seek your advice on selecting a contractor?

12. Does the owner seek your judgment for navigating the entitlement process?

13. In a design-build diagram, does the contractor have you carry the design consultants?

THE CRAFT ADVANTAGE

14 In a design-build diagram, does the contractor allow you to work directly with the owner?

15 Do your clients request your services to help figure out their campus growth?

16 Is your team trusted to lead design coordination meetings? Does your team lead these meetings?

17 Do your clients request that you make presentations representing their project to outside groups?

18 Are you asked to present your work with the owner at a national/regional conference?

19 Are you included in establishing priorities in budget meetings?

20 Are you included in the development of milestone schedule meetings?

21 Does your client or contractor defer design decisions to you and your team?

22 Is your advice requested when the client is confronted with entitlement and jurisdiction challenges?

23 Does the contractor seek your opinion on how to proceed with the city's permitting process?

24 Does your client come to you to learn about design trends in your design sector of expertise?

If you answered "NO" to many of these questions, you are experiencing a reduction in influence.

AUTHOR'S SUMMARY

It will vary by your market sector and your client and contractor relationships, but it can indicate a reduction of influence in any case.

Questions to Consider About Virtual Tools, AI, and the Future

1. Will artificial intelligence (AI) improve design craft or reduce design craft?
2. If exterior design is an export from AI, will that increase the interior experience, design craft, and design influence?
3. Will AI and augmented reality (AR) increase design accountability or reduce it?
4. Will AI and AR decrease design and construction risk?
5. How do we maintain and increase design craft while also taking advantage of the new technology tools? What is the Balance?

AI and a possible future: Imagine in many years: AI is developed to the point where underwriters, owners, municipalities, and the insurance industry support using AI for advanced technical drawings and develop a process of mitigating risk without the primary role of the architect. The architect will have a reduced role, if any role at all, to provide a quality review of the documents, but not be the primary author. If we do not embrace the advantage of craft, we may become the same as the watcher at a six-station self-check-out kiosk station, making sure the bags are open with minimal influence. Maximizing our advantage in craft will be the only resistance to this technology pressure that is sure to arrive sometime in the future.

THE CRAFT ADVANTAGE

THREE COMPONENTS THAT DEFINE THE CRAFT ADVANTAGE

1

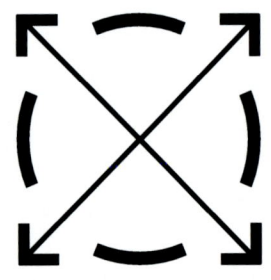

Whole-building thinking and the power of perforated silos

2

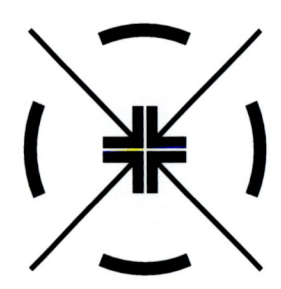

Intelligent idea integration to grow influence

3

Accountability and mentorship by way of follow-through and growth

CRAFT

as a revived core value will increase our influence.

THE MISSION

OPPORTUNITIES AND POSSIBILITIES WITH THE CRAFT ADVANTAGE

High craft will reverse the decline of architecture and improve the built environment. If we organize our disciplines of design, construction, and development into perforated silos that promote interaction between the teams, and if we educate, train, and mentor our architecture students and young professionals to embrace, practice, and deliver quality craftsmanship, we will be able to provide solutions that address the whole design challenge of cost, aesthetics, and function.

It is only then that we will have the best chance of leading our partners by example in the added value of design excellence. Our success will create a culture of increased trust and respect, facilitate more design opportunities, and, over time, improve the built environment one better design decision and opportunity at a time, one after another.

If architects stop looking for comfortable design opportunities, stop following old and diminishing value patterns, stop ignoring the decline, and start focusing on developing integration and craft skills, we will have better success in difficult design environments, the built environment will improve ... and the profession will thrive. It will take time.

OPPORTUNITIES AND POSSIBILITIES

Our profession has been in a slow decline and slipping for many years, and it will take many years to reverse the decline—most likely beyond our own careers. But change can only start once our eyes are open, our gaze is widened, and we turn up the craft dial on excellence, just a little over time, to make a big difference.

Craft as our revived core value will create new opportunities and possibilities that will reverse the craft decline and increase our influence.

OPPORTUNITIES
Craft as a core value will attract clients who value quality craft

RESPECT
Quality follow-through drives respect from clients, colleagues, and partners

REVENUE
More craft means more quality = more projects and revenue

LONGEVITY
More influence and respect = longevity

RELATIONSHIPS
Quality attracts more relationships

INTEGRATION
Better craft requires better integration, which increases quality

HIGHER CRAFT
Higher craft means high quality = fewer errors

LOWER STRESS
Less stress = more fun and time for higher craft

BUILT ENVIRONMENT
Higher craft = high quality, which ripples through everything

INFLUENCE
More craft increases expertise and the number of seats at the table

Isolated examples of great work do very little to improve the overall context. Our success in improving the built environment and increasing influence will depend on a collective action from all levels of our profession to "turn up the craft dial" to improve our craft.

THE MISSION

THE BUILT ENVIRONMENT

A revived core value of craft can improve the built environment, but first, a framework for defining the built environment needs to be established.

As young architecture students, we often hear about the built environment. We hear about how architecture affects the built environment and how it is the architect's responsibility to repair the built environment. But how often has anyone actually defined the built environment or put context around the discussion of the built environment? Not often. Why? Because it is hard to define, it is changing, and when it is undefined, it can be defined to fit whatever design narrative or perspective a person wants to project.

The built environment is what it is. It is a reflection of the history of a neighborhood, it is a reflection of the economics of a region, it is the success of businesses, it is the location of resources and the current building market, and it is a mirror of the culture in that area at that time, before and beyond. The quality of the built environment ranges as much as people, the culture, and their needs and interests range.

What standard is used to measure what is good and what is bad? The standard is usually what we, as architects, like. If we like cutting-edge contemporary architecture, then that is the measure. If we like a European-town look, then that is the measure—and so on and so forth.

To improve our built environment, no matter how it is defined or where it is, we need to establish a fundamental framework of areas to improve that all environments can share and then work to improve the environmental characteristics within that framework.

Otherwise, the idea of improving the built environment will remain elusive and non-effective.

No matter what environmental context the building is in, here are three framework components that can help unify efforts to effectively improve the built environment over time:

1. **Sustainable design.** All built environments can share the goal of sustainable design. No matter where it is, all buildings use some form of energy, pay for that energy, and can benefit from energy efficiency. The Craft Advantage as a core value is about maximizing effectiveness in applied craft within our profession and, by extension, the built environment. Through an efficient and precise integrated design process (increased craft), more project resources can be focused on energy-saving strategies for a building and the region where it is located.

2. **Context improvement contribution.** If architects, in their project designs, contributed more to the urban context, the built environment would improve. For example, add a shade tree near the entrance of a building, add an awning, consider the context to harmonize with or set a standard of improvement for the next building. Many cities enforce this idea through zoning ordinances. The fact that it must be enforced is another example of our reducing influence.

3. **Unity elevated by craft.** If craft becomes a unifying core value in our profession, then it will be hard to find an architect that will accept a reduced standard of quality. If craft remains a shifting priority, then it will be no problem to find an architect that will ignore craft to get the next project. If we are unified in craft as a core value, then the built environment can be improved over time. Divided and it won't change.

There is no easy way, but if this framework can be embraced with craft as a core value, then we have the best chance to improve the built environment; otherwise, it will just remain a convenient talking point to complain about, justify a new style, or just ignore while looking through the straw view.

Unity in craft can empower architects to lead the way with effective design and actually make improvements that matter. Unified in higher craft and greater influence, architects can be the best advocates for a better built environment.

TURN UP THE CRAFT DIAL

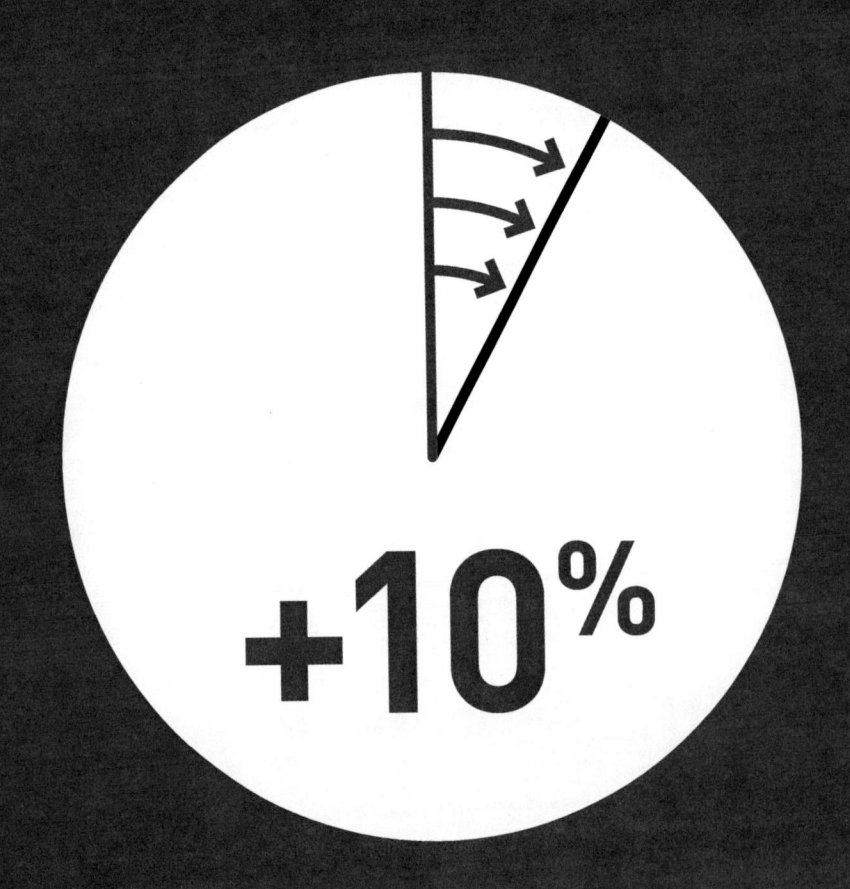

+10%

FOR INCREMENTAL IMPACT OVER TIME

THE BUILT ENVIRONMENT

1

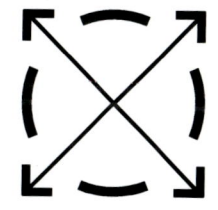

Whole-Building Thinking

Perforate silos to increase whole-building thinking.

TURN UP THE DIAL

Reach out to other disciplines, open your doors to different ideas, embrace diverse thought.

2

Intelligent Idea Integration

Have vision, think hard, and be courageous and creative to increase the integration of intelligent ideas.

TURN UP THE DIAL

Explore more ideas, innovate, break away from conventional thought or convenience to test ideas.

3

Accountability

Mentor, teach, and hold the line on the accountability for quality of craft.

TURN UP THE DIAL

Engage more, take time to mentor, share knowledge and experience, volunteer in education.

THE FRICTION

"Our time is so specialized that we have people who know more and more or less and less."

ALVAR AALTO

THE FRICTION

THE DECLINE TREND AND THE SKEPTICAL ARCHITECT

As an architecture student, I was very skeptical and didn't believe anything that would suggest a decline in our profession. If anything, I believed that architects are, without question, essential. But are we? Do we act essential? Is our influence great? Do we own a role that is considered essential by others in our industry? Do we even see a decline? I don't think so. We are too busy with the straw view, and many of us are just trying to stay alive in the profession. We are romanced by the exceptions in our profession and blind to the inertia of the decline of craft and the resultant reduction of influence.

The following are my three primary observations to consider:

1. We have created a void, as the result of a decline in quality and craft, that our industry partners are filling with "architect replacement expertise," which reduces our influence.

2. Our ability to integrate design with vision at a high level of craft can and should be a revived core value to increase influence.

3. Our greatest opportunity for greater influence to improve the built environment and have a positive influence in our industry is to celebrate architecture by protecting the architecture profession through excellence in craft.

Dialogue with a "Skeptical Architect"

SKEPTICAL ARCHITECT "I don't see a reduction in craft or reduced influence or any notable decline. I see some architects not doing great work, but other architects are doing amazing work. An overall decline in craft and influence in the profession? I don't see it."

ME "It is true that there are exceptional architects doing exceptional work, but they are the exception to the rule. The majority of the profession is driven by the rule and not the exceptions that are celebrated in the architecture media, by universities, at award ceremonies, and at national and regional meetings. We get enjoyment and inspiration from the exceptions, but when the inspiration wears off, we are left with only a very few doing exceptional work, the vast majority doing acceptable but average work, and many doing below-average work—not enough to turn the dial in the right direction."

THE DECLINE TREND AND THE SKEPTICAL ARCHITECT

SKEPTICAL ARCHITECT "We are guided by the exceptional work. It is where we learn and get that inspiration you mention. It is how great architecture happens."

ME "My point is that, great and inspiring work aside, the majority of work creates the inertia that drives the profession and the quality of the built environment. Drive down any street in America and count how many average buildings there are and how many inspiring buildings there are. Excellence is outnumbered by the average many times over."

SKEPTICAL ARCHITECT "True, but isn't that why the exceptional work is important to be the inspiration to change the majority of the work?!"

ME "In an ideal setting, of course, but the reality is that the inertia I mention is massive, and it is why the dream of a better built environment never seems to happen. The inertia of the average is just too big and the exceptional architecture just too small."

SKEPTICAL ARCHITECT "I see this, but isn't the better approach to focus on the exceptional work and why the work is exceptional and use those lessons to improve the built environment?"

ME "I think the lessons from the exceptional work are as important as the lessons from the average and below-average work—maybe even less so. If you consider that the majority of the work is average at best, then doesn't it make sense to spend more time learning the lessons of *why* it is average so that we can learn how to improve the work that is having the largest impact on the built environment? Don't you think?"

SKEPTICAL ARCHITECT "I see your point."

ME "To expand a little further, it is often the case that some architects need certain ideal variables in place to engage the effort to turn an average design opportunity into an exceptional design opportunity. For example, these variables could include having a big budget, a supportive contractor, and an owner with an interest in a higher design aesthetic. Because these variables can be difficult to find in many project opportunities all at once, we need to look harder at what is available that can be amplified into better-quality design. Some architects, when they don't see the ideal variables, tend to turn a blind eye and say, 'Well, next time, when we have a better situation …' This is why the average work creates more inertia within the quality of the built environment."

SKEPTICAL ARCHITECT "So the average work wins over time?"

ME "Only if we don't change our trajectory. It is dramatically harder to create beauty from less-ideal circumstances than from more ideal circumstances. It requires more skill. The Craft Advantage is about elevating our skills to be able to maximize the smaller variables, where we find them, into bigger design opportunities within the project. It is like shooting an arrow at a target: more skill, better score. With more precision in our craft skill, we can elevate and maximize the smaller, less-ideal variables into better-than-average work. Each time we turn up the dial just a little, the built environment gets better and our influence increases."

SKEPTICAL ARCHITECT "What makes you think our influence is diminishing?"

ME "The best evidence of the decrease in our influence is watching what the contractors are doing. Our drop in craft has increased their risk. They don't like risk. Instead of waiting for us to improve while they deal with profit erosion and reduced efficiency, they are filling the craft vacuum we have created with, as I called it, 'architect replacement expertise' tools, virtual design and construction coordination teams, and software coordination tools to offset the risk."

SKEPTICAL ARCHITECT "I didn't realize this was happening. What happened?"

THE DECLINE TREND AND THE SKEPTICAL ARCHITECT

ME "I think that with our reaction to an accelerated market and the need to move quicker, architects embraced the new virtual drawing tools to increase efficiency, but what wasn't realized at the time was that the power within these virtual tools did not include craft, only efficiency. We sped forward without integrating our traditional value of craft into the use of the new virtual drawing tools. We just assumed that craft was our default quality because it was so intrinsic to our culture. We didn't even notice that it was slipping—the slip was so slow. The slip, combined with the accelerated change in our culture, resulted in less time to teach and mentor, less time to follow up on drawing coordination to ensure quality, less time to ensure that we have the best details, and less time to influence quality in the built environment. The slip created a craft vacuum that the contractor had no choice but to fill, resulting in our reduced influence."

SKEPTICAL ARCHITECT "Wow, this makes sense, but the problem I am still having with this is that I am still seeing quality projects happening."

ME "What you are not seeing is risk and profit loss that the contractor is having to absorb. What I have learned from my experience working with many contractors is that they don't advertise their struggles; they just find ways to fix the challenges. It is very impressive, by the way."

SKEPTICAL ARCHITECT "Point understood but not liked. How can you assume that the contractors are doing more of what architects are doing? They are not creating the design documents."

ME "Very true. They are not, but essentially they are finishing the effort that we didn't finish. As is often the case, the person who finishes what was started gets the most credit and influence. Also, I am not assuming—I am relaying experience. I have seen it happening for many years. To answer your question more clearly, let me first ask you a question: What do you think is the primary mission for the builder?"

SKEPTICAL ARCHITECT "To build what we design per our design documents."

THE CRAFT ADVANTAGE

ME "Nope, it is to reduce their risk in building our design from our design documents. Do you think that architects reduce or increase a builder's risk?"

SKEPTICAL ARCHITECT "It depends on the builder, I guess, but if I had to pick one, I would say that we reduce their risk because even with imperfect drawings, they would have more risk without them."

ME "So you are saying 'better than nothing'? It is true that it depends on the builder, but the design quality starts with the architect's value of craft and quality. We set the tone, and we set the risk profile by our follow-through, or a lack thereof. Do you think the profession is generally producing higher or less-resolved drawings? Are the details better resolved? Are the drawings better coordinated? Are the drawings being reviewed and refined by experienced architects with many years of constructability knowledge? Not as much anymore. We increase the builder's risk by having incomplete and less-developed drawings, or, better put, incomplete instructions to build the building."

SKEPTICAL ARCHITECT "I get it, but why is this apparently not seen by many in our industry?"

ME "I think it is seen by some, but everyone is so busy trying to stay relevant and afloat. This, combined with a tendency toward the straw view, makes it become not easily noticed, but with a wider gaze, it is clear. I know, like you know, that if you widen your gaze, you will see it for yourself. Here is the deal: We have less time to spend on drawings because schedules have been compressed. We have less-skilled graduates because school accreditation drives a fragmented checklist approach to building design and an integrated whole-building perspective. We have less-experienced and fewer constructability tested architects to mentor the next generation and less time to mentor and constructively elevate the performance of our team members to increase learning and drawing quality. Any principal architect will tell you that finding a great senior technical architect is extremely hard."

THE DECLINE TREND AND THE SKEPTICAL ARCHITECT

SKEPTICAL ARCHITECT "So what is the best path forward, and what should be the ultimate mission?"

ME "If a contractor's prime mission is to reduce risk, then our mission needs to be to reduce risk by increasing the quality of our craft. If we do this, the contractor will no longer need to fill the craft void because the void will diminish."

SKEPTICAL ARCHITECT "It's that simple? Just increase the quality?"

ME "Yes, the mission is simple. The path forward to achieve the mission will be very hard. A common saying to remember is 'it is easier to fall into a hole then to get out of the hole.' It will take incredible effort and unity by architects to reverse the decline. The effort may be too much, but I think it can and will happen if we want it to happen. Our challenge is heightened by the fact that the contractor has spent a lot of money and taken time to develop the skills and acquire the tools to try to fill the gap. Those tools and teams will not go away because we start to improve our craft, but the need will diminish over time as we increase the quality. As our influence grows, their influence will level out, and we will be on par once again and a better team."

SKEPTICAL ARCHITECT "I see. I have one more question, will AI replace architects?"

ME "Yes, if we continue to relinquish accountability. While AI is not far enough along in development to create safe, thorough, and fully integrated design documents, it is trending in that direction. The one thing that AI can't do is assume risk and ownership. Once we give up owning the risk and AI advances to the point where the industry develops a framework to "trust" AI on assuming risk, then our influence will drop to the point of being a novelty more than a necessity. Maximizing craft is our advantage to resist this trend."

THE DECLINE SEQUENCE TOWARD REDUCED INFLUENCE

1 In the 1970s, the idea of accelerated change, written about in Alvin Toffler's book *Future Shock*, became a part of societal awareness, driving an increased need for market speed. In the 1980s, this idea drove an increased need to create efficiency and speed within the process of drawing the design for a building. This need created the rise and implementation of virtual drawing tools.

2 With traditional drawing, skills were evident and easily visible to senior architects. Virtual tools hide craft "skill" behind a screen that tends to obscure visibility of deficits in skill. While virtual tools improve convenience, they also increase the potential for a reduction in skill growth and quality accountability. You can't fix or improve what is not easily seen.

3 When skill, quality, and accountability are reduced, a craft void is created that is filled with increased risk. This risk reveals itself in more change orders for the client, wasted time in the field, less safety in the field, lower-quality details and building construction, more profit erosion, and reputational damage for both the architect and contractor.

4 Over time, as the craft void gets bigger, it requires the contractor to continue to fill the void with "architect replacement expertise" to offset their risk exposure and profit erosion.

THE NEGATIVE EFFECTS

» Speed requires more skill to maintain quality. Quality as a core value got lost as architects tried to adapt to the increased need for speed with virtual drawing tools that can increase efficiency at the expense of craft. Skill and quality dropped as speed increased.

» Quality decreases when accountability is reduced. Speed, combined with document quality that is obscured by the virtual interface, leaves less time to see deficits and less time to correct, if corrected at all.

» The increased risk originates from the architect. The architect sets the tone for the project risk profile. The contractor has to deal with the increased risk. The contractor reduces this risk by filling the craft void with new tools and people to manage the risk.

» As the void grows and craft declines, the contractor's influence increases while the architect's influence decreases. Less influence, reduced fees, less impact.

THE FRICTION

THE DECLINE TREND: INTRODUCTION

With reduced influence, how can we advance the architecture profession so it can continue to thrive amid and survive the future changes in the design, build, and development industry?

How can we become the essential ingredient in any project pursuit so that contractors, developers, and owners are willing to pay top dollar for the services and listen more to the advice of the architect?

How do we reset the table so that architects are top valued and not devalued?

The decline trend is directly the result of a decline in craft as a core value. When craft declines, our value declines and our influence declines.

Architects reinforce being devalued by not living up to the responsibility of craft, having the "straw view", by being more concerned with our own vanity, by ignoring the drop in quality of deliverables, by not getting involved in the education of our future architects, by allowing the contractor to fill the craft void left by architects with "architect replacement expertise," for not valuing the contractor's risk by providing

THE DECLINE TREND: INTRODUCTION

beautifully coordinated drawings, and, quite simply, by not attempting to be better than anyone in our industry. We should want the builder and developer to say, "If we want accuracy, quality, and effectiveness, we need an architect on our team."

Architects have allowed the idea that anyone can do what we do. This is getting amplified by new technology, home improvement apps, and computational design. If we don't change the trajectory of our profession, people will be able to go through the self-checkout at some retailer to get their design documents.

What we need to do is refocus on enhancing the craft of architecture to the point where no one will dare look for an easy way to get architectural services. The value of the built environment is too important, and the architect should be the Lorax (Dr. Seuss) of the built environment. When we are, we will have reversed our current trajectory of decline.

The decline trend is going unnoticed by many architects that are too busy to notice what to fix or even that there is a problem. We are an interesting group, no doubt. We are precise. We are passionate. We are artists. We are engineers. We are scientists. We tend to have unique insights, but I think that architects are made to be slightly delusional so that we can be creative without too much of the burden of reality. Instead of focusing on the essence of beauty built, integration with our industry partners, and enhancing our craft, our profession is leaning toward saving ourselves and not the profession. While we act as individual islands, we tend to ignore the ocean around us. We need our "ocean" healthy so our islands can flourish. One supports the other. If our craft is high, the profession is healthy and strong. When

THE CRAFT ADVANTAGE

our craft is low, budgets are blown and relationships are impacted; fewer people will listen to us. If we want to have an effective impact on the profession, the built environment, and the world, we need to refocus inwardly on excellence in craft and delivery. We need to remaster the basics of craft and redefine craft for our time to grow our influence. When our influence grows, our influence on the macro scale of social and environmental issues will grow. The reality is that there is no "fixing the world" without a national level of respect and without individual standards of high craft and skill. Craft as a core value can unite our entire architecture profession.

When we own the advantage of craft, we will have earned respect from our industry partners and have a national audience that will listen and be more receptive to our ideas of improvement, sustainable design, universal design, and, overall, improving the experience in the built environment.

THE DECLINE TREND: INTRODUCTION

To improve, we need to keep in mind the primary drivers behind the decline in craft and skill, which are, in summary:

- → Accelerated change and technology
- → Increased need for speed
- → The need and adoption of virtual drawing tools to increase efficiency
- → Virtual drawing tools make skill deficits harder to see
- → Hard to improve skill in staff when the deficits are harder to see
- → Speed requires more skill to maintain quality
- → Speed offers less time to mentor staff to craft drawings and design
- → Quality drops when accountability drops
- → The craft void is created by architects and increases risk for architects and contractors
- → The contractor fills the void with "architect replacement expertise," new staff, and software
- → While the void grows, the contractor's influence increases, filling the craft void
- → The architect's influence decreases over time as craft declines and the contractor's influence grows

The diagrams on the following pages illustrate the phases, pressures, curves, and inflection points of the reduction of influence and the potential to increase craft and influence.

THE DECLINE TREND
PHASES

Influence

A Craft, once as a core value; more time, more quality, more influence

B Straw view; craft is in decline with no resistance; reduced influence and quality

C Craft as revived core value; quality and influence increase over time

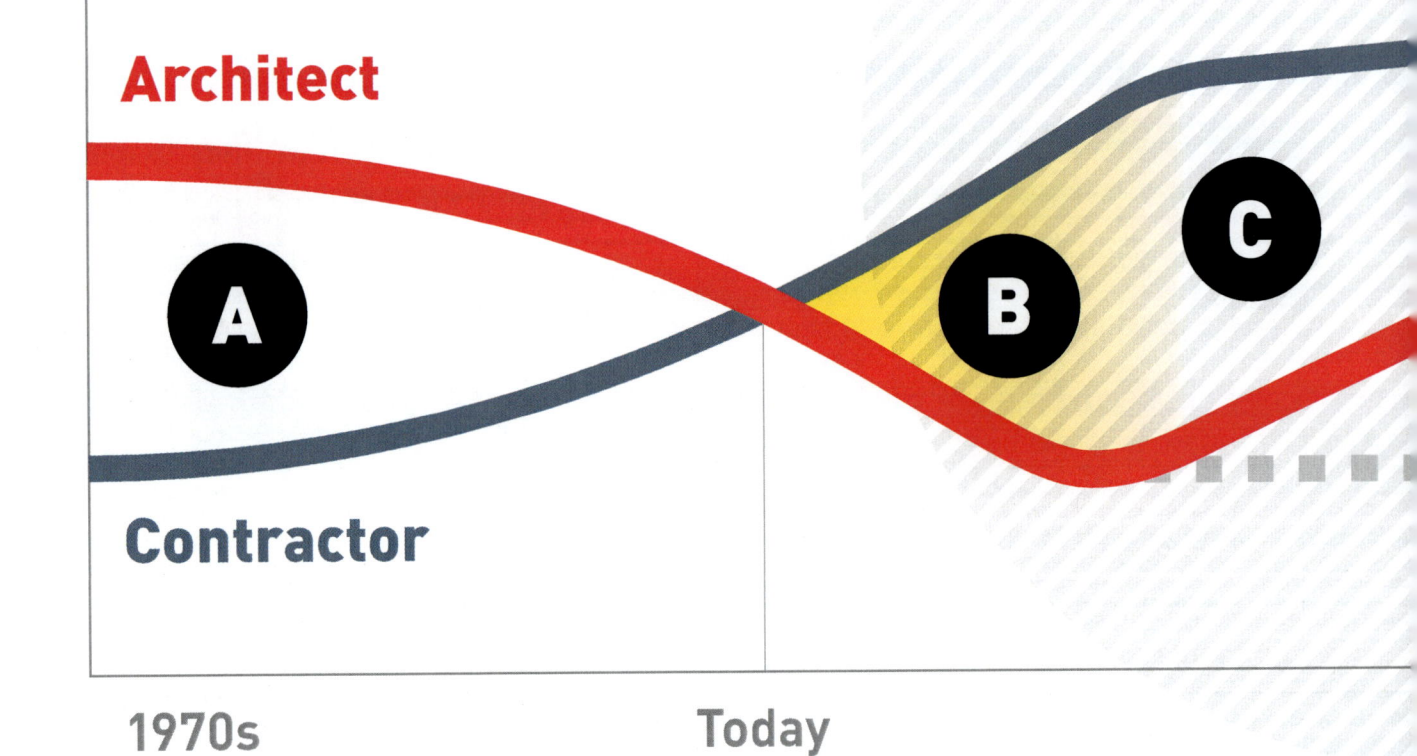

Architect

Contractor

1970s — Today

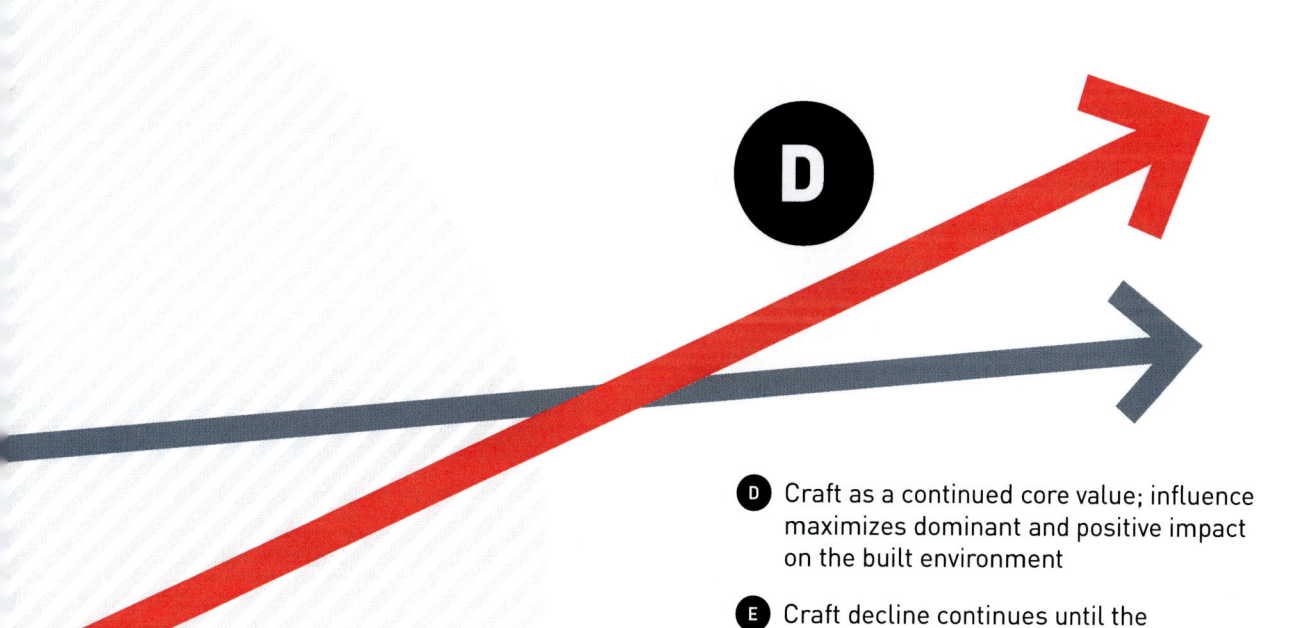

D Craft as a continued core value; influence maximizes dominant and positive impact on the built environment

E Craft decline continues until the architect's influence reduces to a drafting service role or replaced by AI, resulting in a reduced ability to improve the built environment and our profession.

THE DECLINE TREND
INFLECTION POINTS

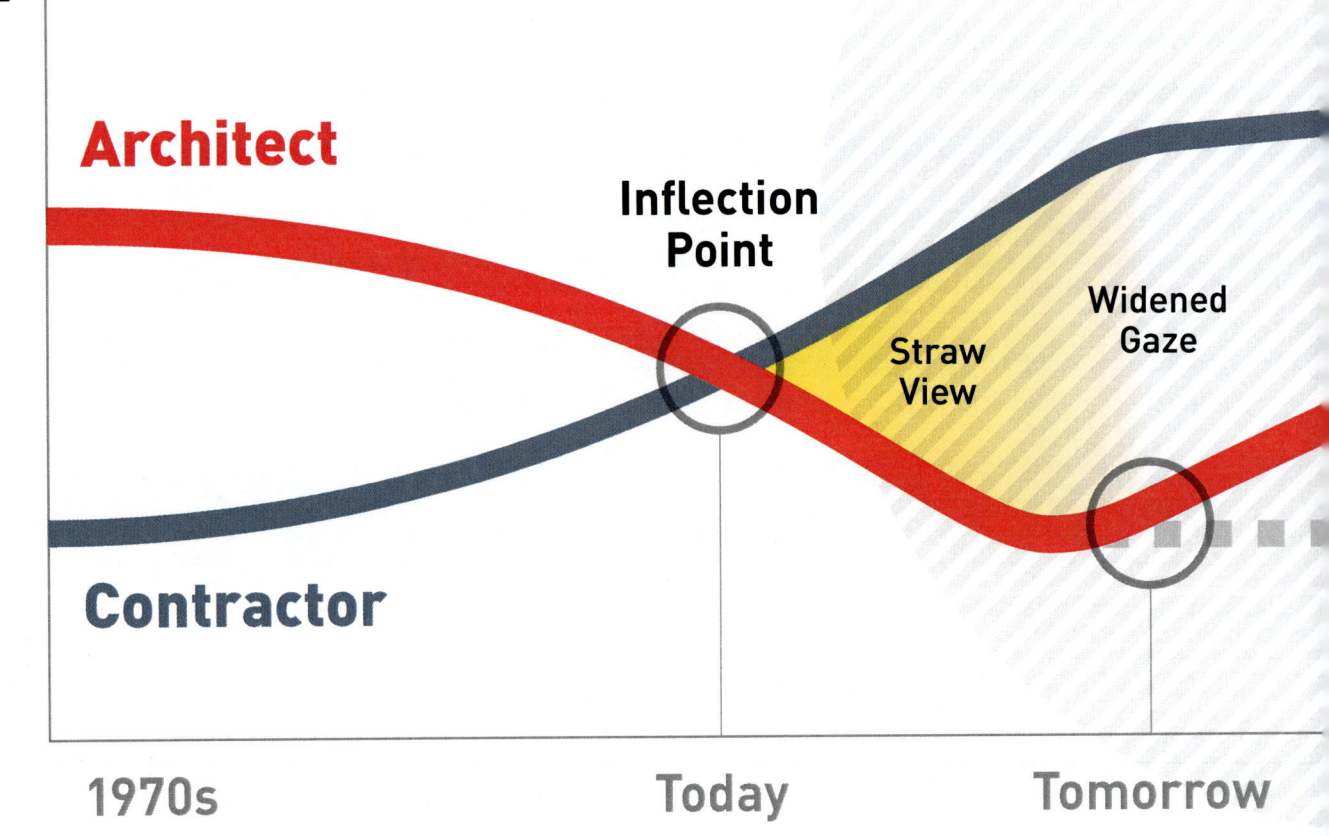

Influence

Architect

Inflection Point

Straw View

Widened Gaze

Contractor

1970s   Today   Tomorrow

Craft Revived

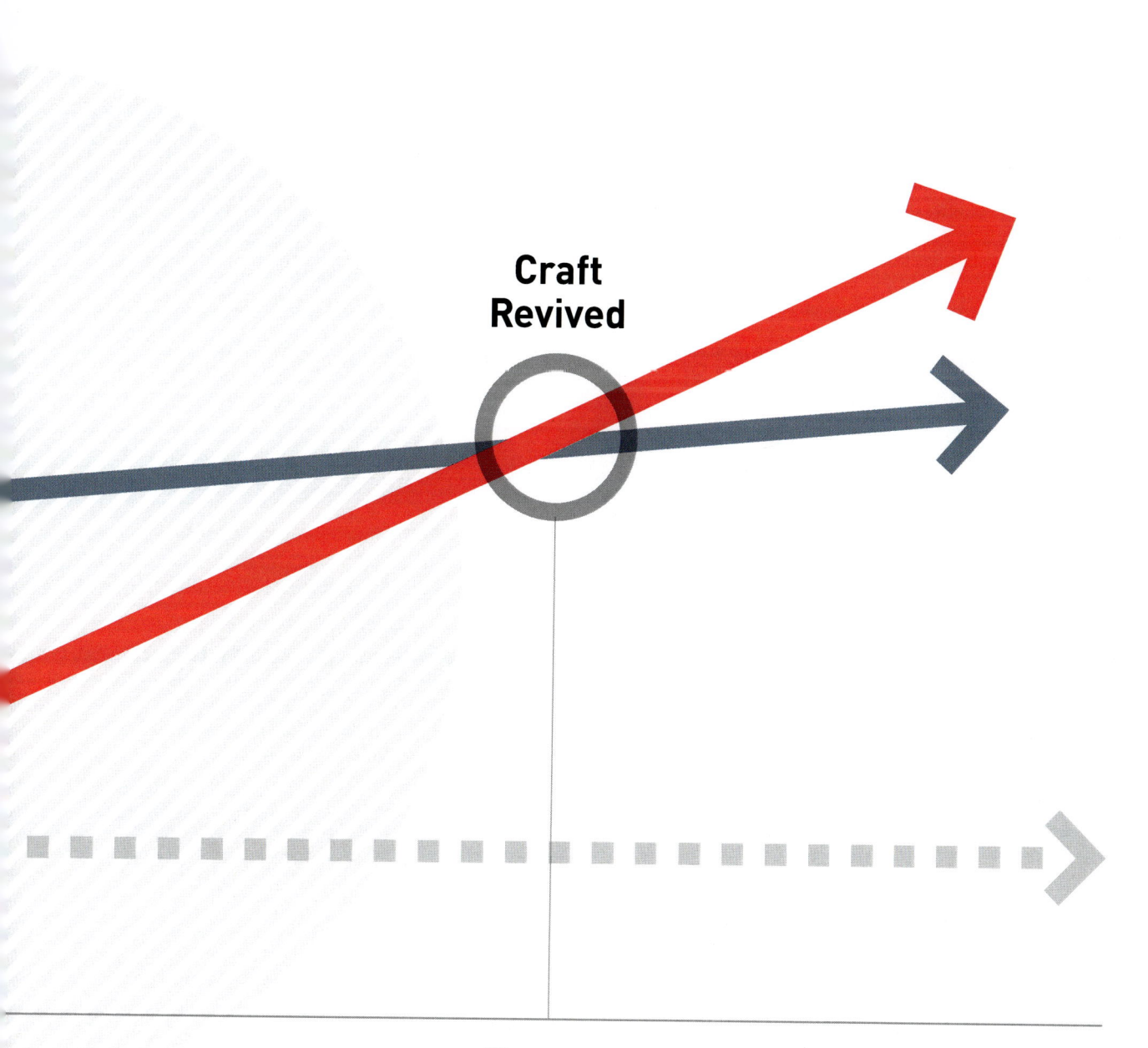

Future

THE DECLINE TREND
CURVES AND PRESSURES

1 **Decline in knowledge about the whole building:** Accelerated change resulted in less time available to increase knowledge across disciplines and building expertise.

2 **Decline in idea influence:** Moving quicker without increased craft reduced available time to generate vision and new ideas across disciplines. When idea quality drops, then the confidence in the architect's input and counsel drops.

3 **Decline in detail craft and accountability:** Reduced technical skill and mentorship as the result of an increased reliance on virtual tools for a perceived increased time efficiency without the required increase in technical skill to maintain quality at a faster delivery. We are moving faster at the expense of craft quality.

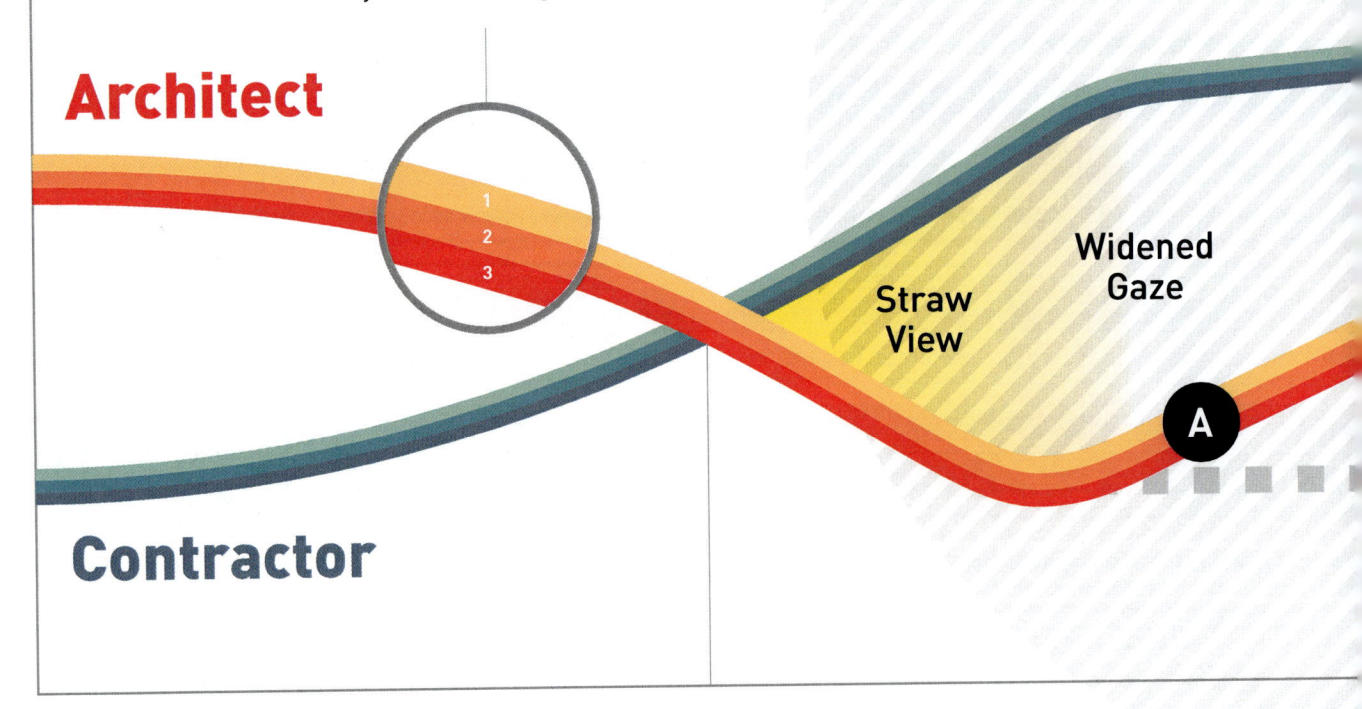

Influence

Architect

Contractor

Straw View

Widened Gaze

A

1970s

Today

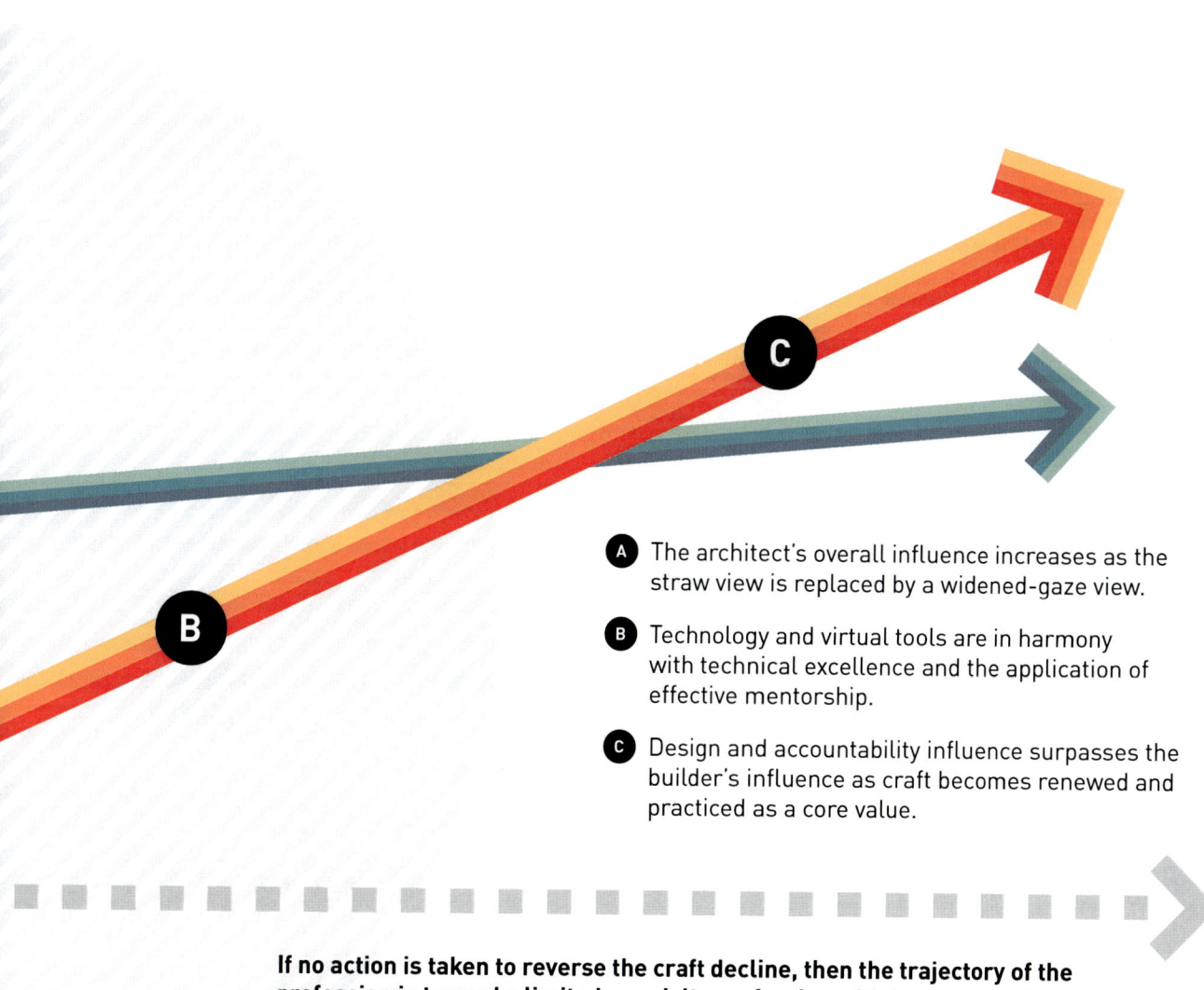

A The architect's overall influence increases as the straw view is replaced by a widened-gaze view.

B Technology and virtual tools are in harmony with technical excellence and the application of effective mentorship.

C Design and accountability influence surpasses the builder's influence as craft becomes renewed and practiced as a core value.

If no action is taken to reverse the craft decline, then the trajectory of the profession is toward a limited-specialty profession with less responsibility being led by the those with maximum responsibility: the builders.

THE DECLINE TREND
CURVES AND PRESSURES

1. **Increase in contractor risk:** Accelerated schedules and poor architecture craft increases the contractor's risk in building the project.

2. **Increase in the contractor's influence:** As the contractor fills the craft void left by the architect, the contractor's influence on the design process increases. The architect's design influence decreases as confidence is reduced in the architect's ability to deliver consistent quality.

3. **Increased adoption of virtual drawing and coordination tools by the contractor:** The contractor adds "architect replacement expertise" to reduce risk prior to building the building. Because the architect is not crafting great documents, the builder has no choice but to do it for the architect to reduce their own risk.

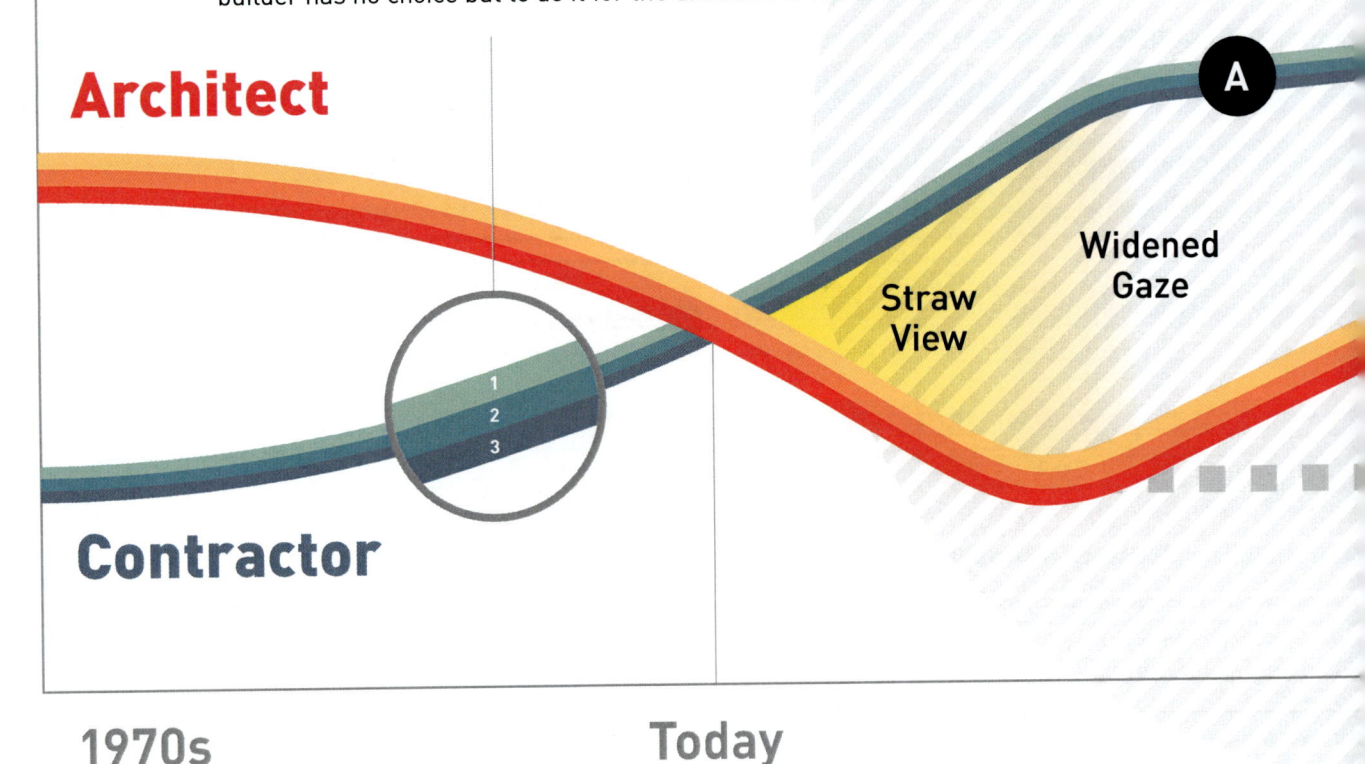

Influence

Architect

Contractor

Straw View

Widened Gaze

A

1970s

Today

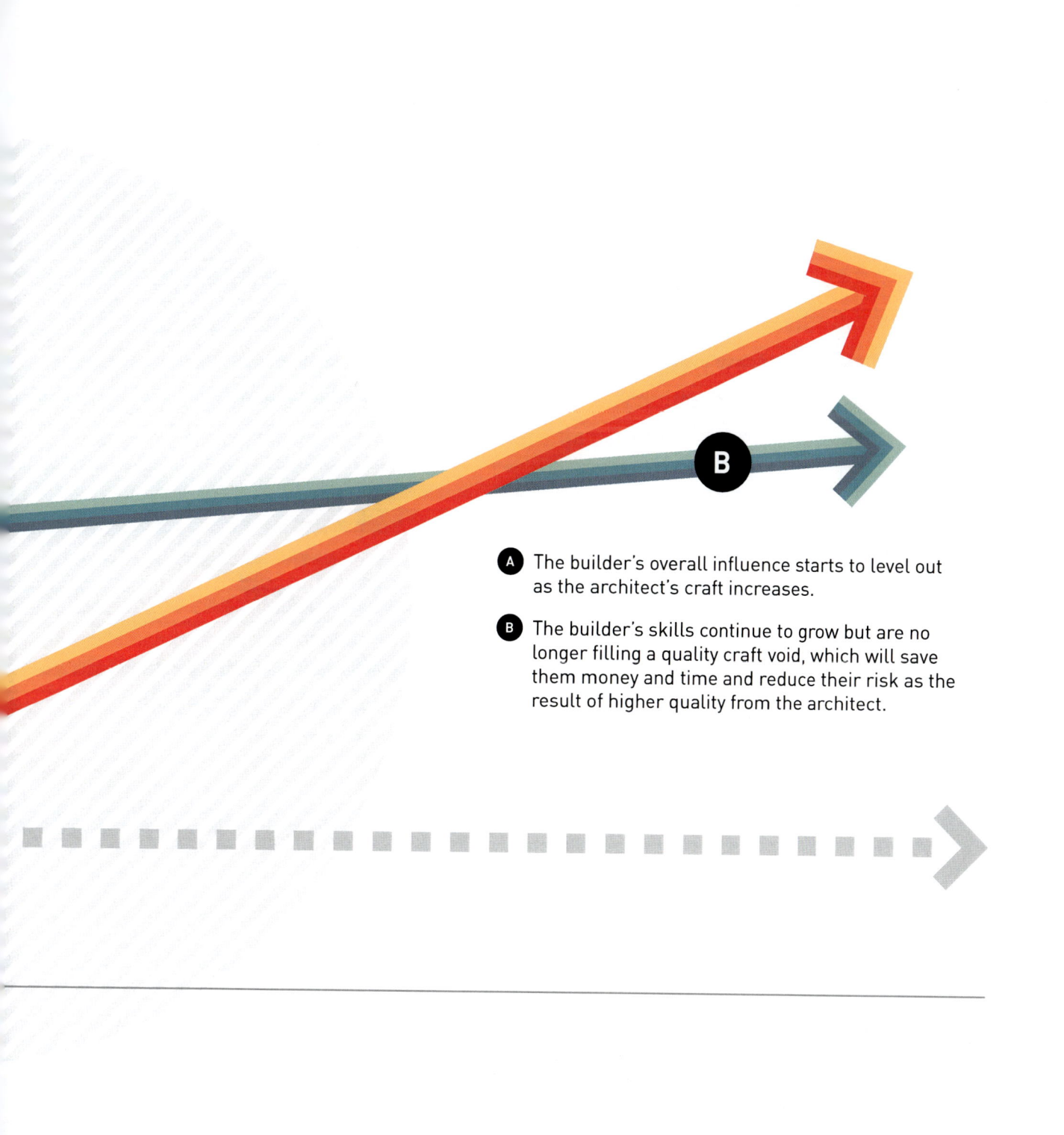

A The builder's overall influence starts to level out as the architect's craft increases.

B The builder's skills continue to grow but are no longer filling a quality craft void, which will save them money and time and reduce their risk as the result of higher quality from the architect.

THE DECLINE TREND
TODAY

Influence

TODAY: We are at the inflection crossover. The inertia of ignoring the reality of the decline is the driving downward force on the curve. The straw view is the dominant perspective, but a widened gaze with unified action will begin to replace the straw view with a broader commitment to craft.

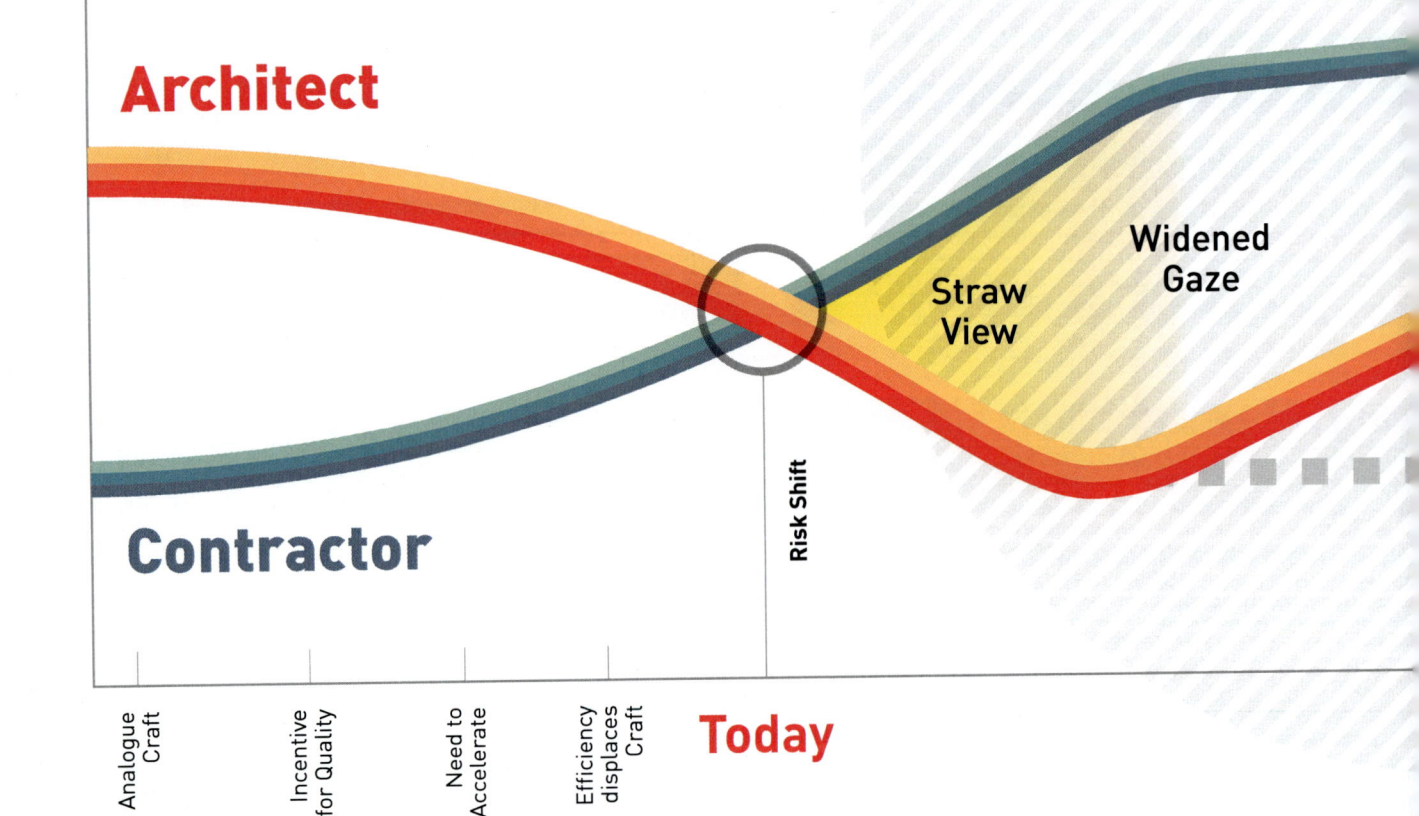

Architect

Contractor

Straw View

Widened Gaze

Risk Shift

Analogue Craft · Incentive for Quality · Need to Accelerate · Efficiency displaces Craft · **Today**

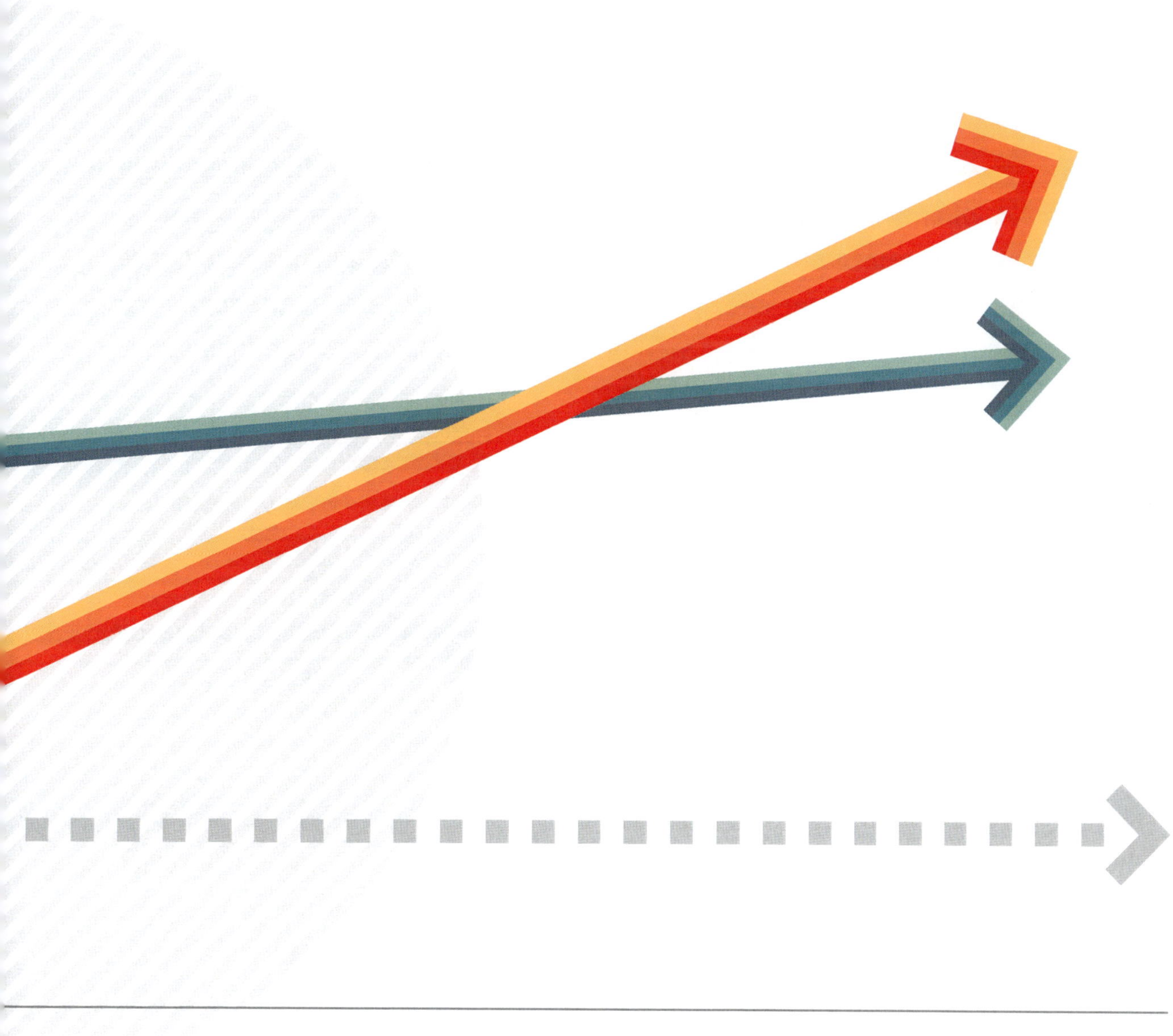

THE DECLINE TREND
TOMORROW

TOMORROW: We can be at the decline reversal inflection point. This is when the decline inertia from the straw view is replaced with a widened-gaze perspective, combined with action, pushing the curve upward. This is the decision point: the crossroads between excellence in craft and influence or mediocrity moving toward insignificance.

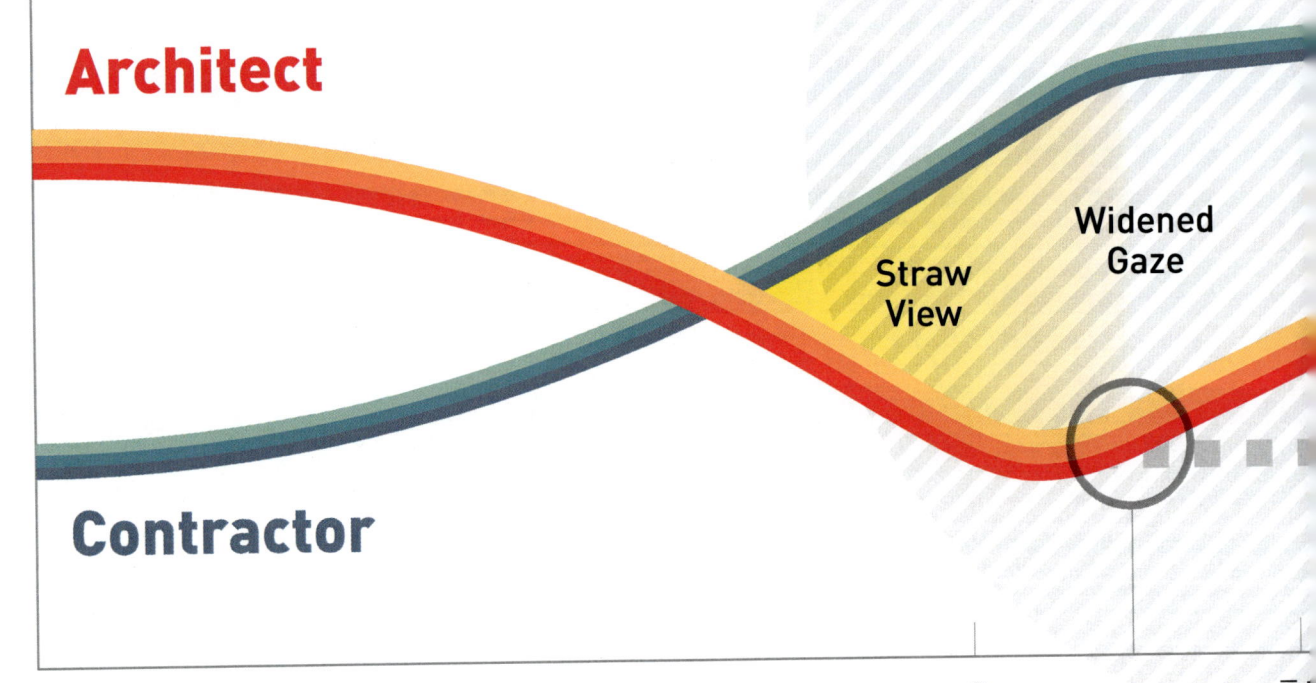

Influence

Architect

Straw View

Widened Gaze

Contractor

AI Pressure

Tomorrow

Integrate AI

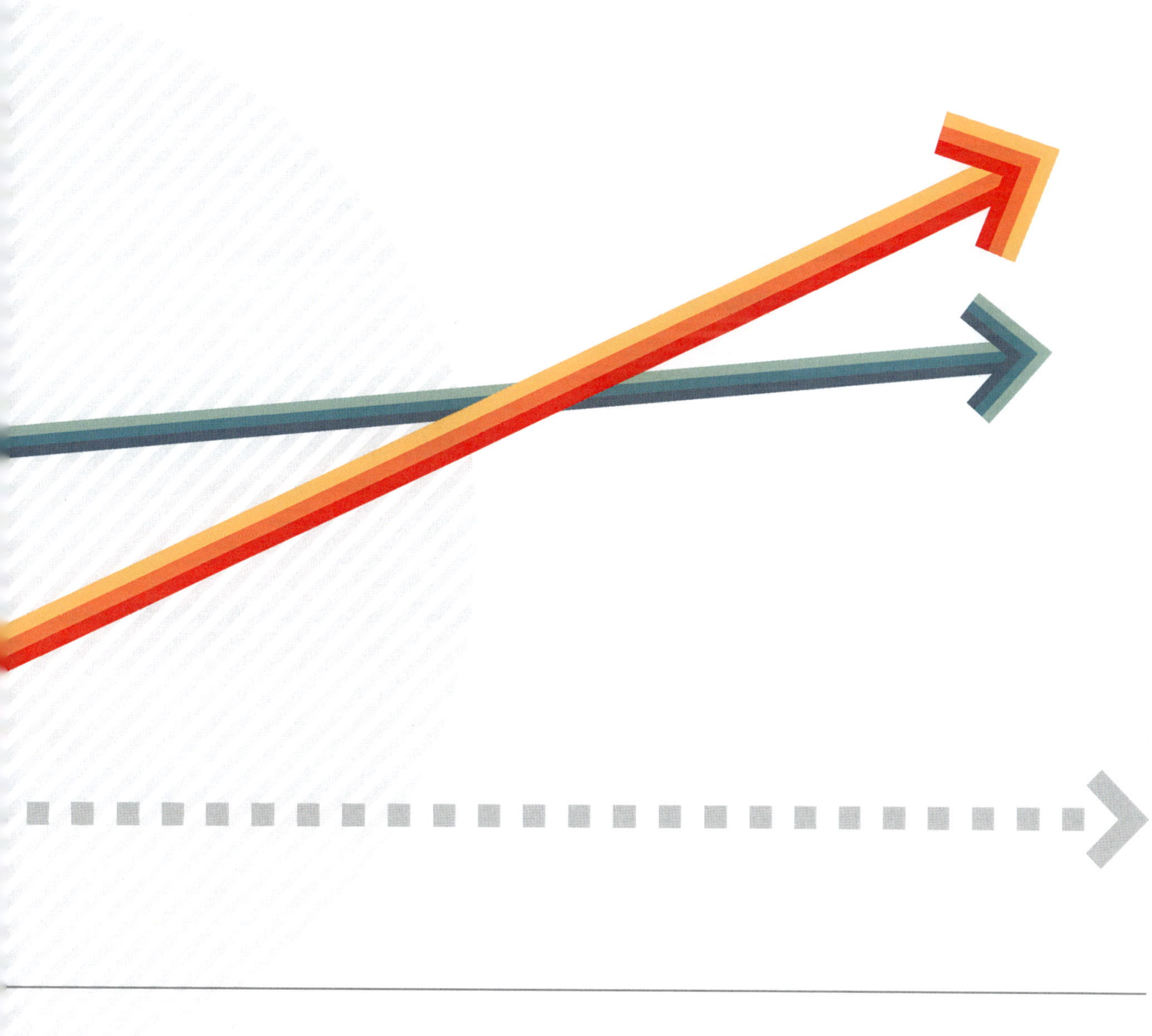

THE POSSIBILITY TREND
THE FUTURE

FUTURE: Lasting impact and dominant influence for a better built environment, overall quality of architecture, and sustainability within a diverse society. Architects become essential and relied upon as leaders for a better world.

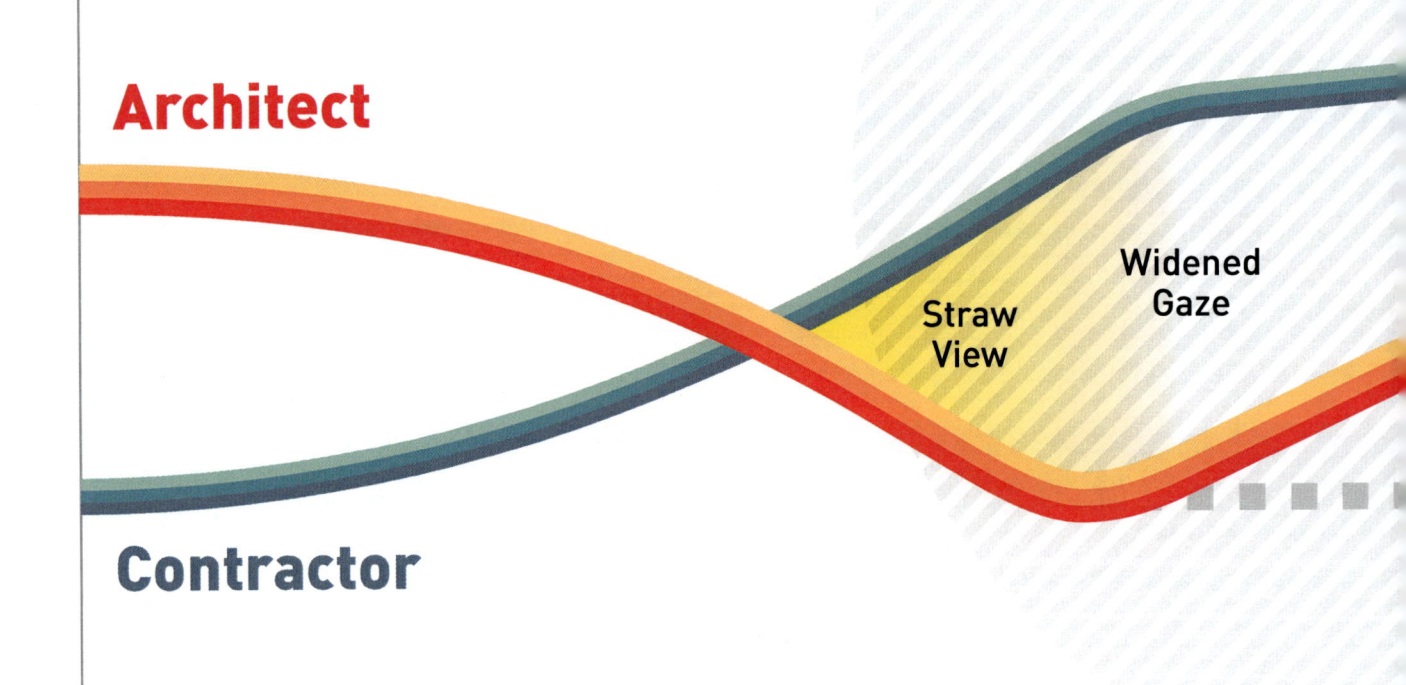

Influence

Architect

Straw View

Widened Gaze

Contractor

Craft Revived

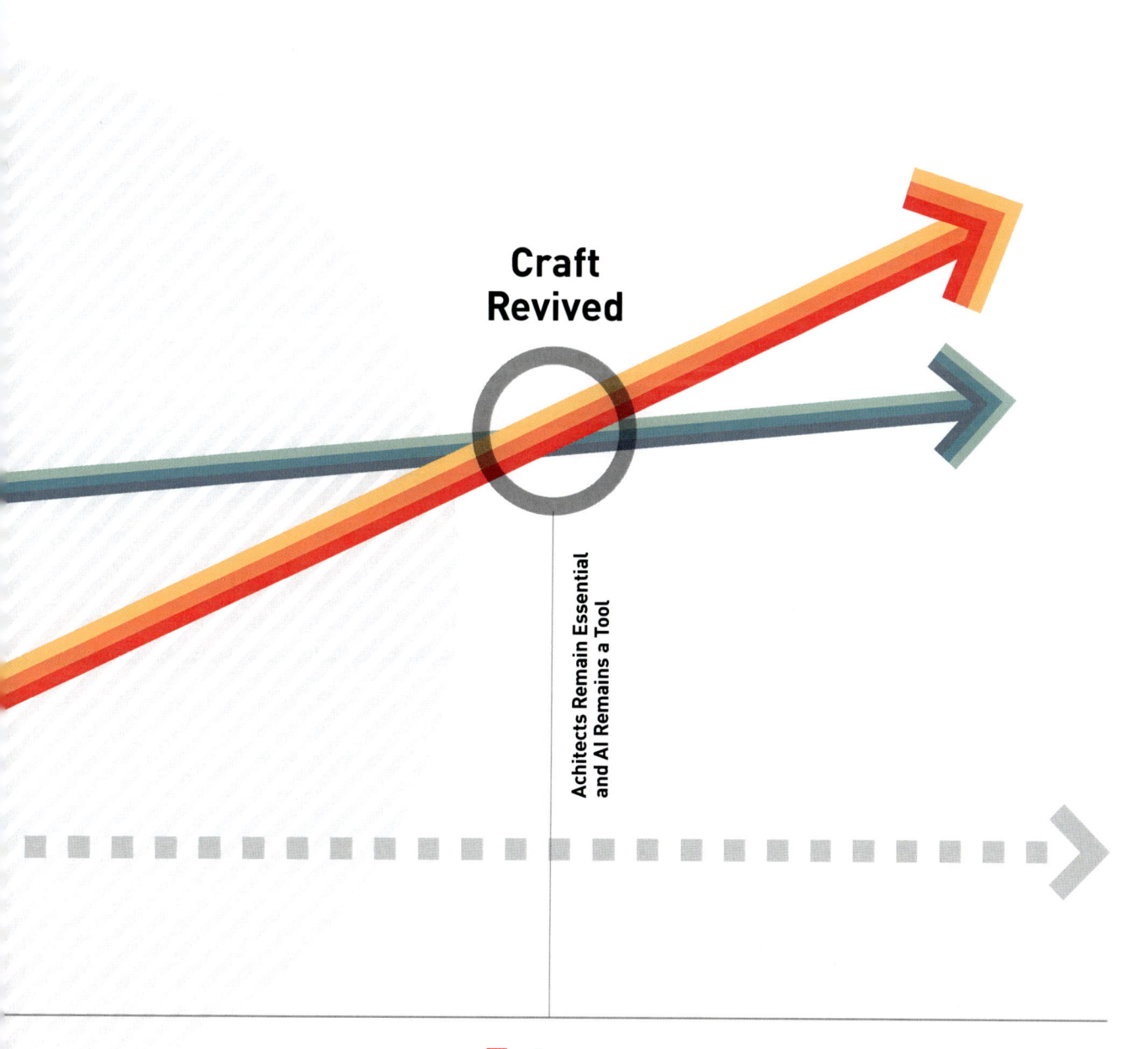

Achitects Remain Essential and AI Remains a Tool

Future

THE MECHANICS TO REVERSE THE DECLINE AND GROW INFLUENCE

1 The decline is fed by a reduction in whole-building thinking and the resistance of cross-discipline collaboration (i.e., resisting perforated silos). This is further amplified by the reduction in available time in an accelerated delivery market.

2 The influence decline involves reduced idea influence and idea integration as the result of accelerated delivery and less time available to integrate across disciplines and expertise. When idea quality drops, then the confidence in the architect's input and counsel drops.

3 The decline in detail craft and accountability involves reduced technical skill and mentorship and reliance on virtual tools to offset the decrease in time without increasing technical skill required to maintain quality at a faster delivery; this shifts risk to the builder. Details are less resolved, less understood, and technically underdeveloped.

4 The downward pressure as the result of decline mechanics is resisted by embracing the Craft Advantage of whole-building thinking, intelligent idea integration, and accountability.

THE POSITIVE EFFECTS

» **Whole-Building Thinking (and the Power of Perforated Silos)**
1. Learn Everything
2. Perforated Silos: Learn What Matters to Others
3. Engage in and Complete the "Circle"
4. Detail Excellence = Whole-Building Excellence
5. Enhanced Communication and Coordination

» **Intelligent Idea Integration (Growing Influence)**
1. Infinite Ideas: The Design Superpower
2. Concept, Brand, and Story
3. Horizon Seeking
4. Success Empathy
5. The Integration State of Mind

» **Accountability and Mentorship (Follow-Through and Growth)**
1. Professional Accountability
2. Personal Accountability
3. Practice Accountability
4. Mentorship
5. Volunteering and Community

» As the Craft Advantage is practiced and mentored, the architect's influence will increase. More influence, more fees, more impact.

THE SKILLS

"We shape our buildings; thereafter they shape us."

WINSTON CHURCHILL

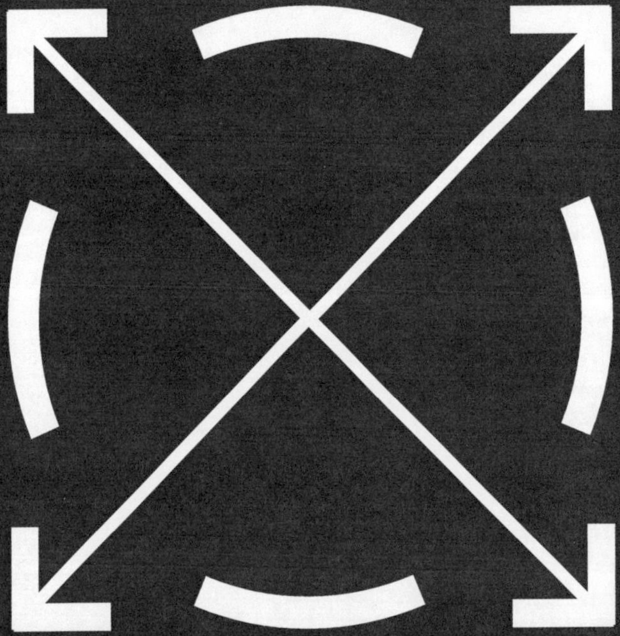

THE SKILLS

WHOLE-BUILDING THINKING (AND THE POWER OF PERFORATED SILOS)

With this quote in mind, shouldn't we, as architects, do everything we can to train ourselves, our teams, our students, and our industry partners to consider all aspects of the whole building? If what we do has such an impact, why would we not make it a point to learn the whole building and become experts in all aspects of the building: the budget, systems, construction, interior design, exterior envelope, landscape, energy and sustainability, codes, universal design, brand, image, and politics? Very few, in my experience, are experts in many of these areas. We delegate to consultant experts to save time and money and shift risk. If we want to regain our influence and reverse the decline, we need to recapture the whole-building expertise. It will require practicing the Craft Advantage, having a widened-gaze view, and collaborating through perforated silos of expertise in order to achieve mastery of the whole building.

Whole-building thinking is the first craft skill required to reverse the decline.

It is made up of the following five topics:

1. Learn Everything
2. Perforated Silos : Learn What Matters to Others
3. Engage in and Complete the "Circle"
4. Detail Excellence = Whole-Building Excellence
5. Enhanced Communication and Coordination

Learn Everything

Learning is an attitude. Many people with a great deal of knowledge are behind a successful project. Take advantage of all that knowledge and experience to learn everything you can about the whole building. *Learn everything* means learn what they know—not necessarily all the details or calculations, per se, but the principles of what they do, the pressures that they are burdened with to do their job, and what defines success for them. Understand your engineer's design process: Where do they start? What do they need from the architects to be more efficient? Ask questions of the contractors and subcontractors and find out what drives their process. Learn the details when it makes sense. Understand how the electrical systems work, learn how the heating, ventilating, and air-conditioning (HVAC) system works. Develop detailed knowledge of the various constraints so that you can be better at design collaboration with the extended team. Learn more to contribute more to the solutions. With more overall knowledge, combined with the architect's natural creativity, better solutions can be found and integrated into the whole-building solution.

There are two categories that I think apply to this goal:

1. **Learning everything about your industry partners' constraints.** Learning about your industry partners' constraints is as simple as caring enough to ask. Ask the following questions: "What keeps you up at night about your mission?" "What is your favorite aspect of your job?" "What are your personal goals for this project?" "What are the expectations from your leaders?" Or, best yet, ask, "How can I help, and what can I change to help you succeed?" Each of these questions will achieve two things: (1) They will break down communication barriers, which will build a relationship and the required reciprocal knowledge sharing. (2) You will learn.

2. **Learning everything about the industry and beyond.** If you can become a lifelong learner, you will find continuous joy in our profession. I love architecture because every project is a new experience involving new people, new knowledge, new challenges, new adventures, and new learning. It amazes me. To be a lifelong learner means to be always curious and inquisitive by asking questions, thinking about the answers, asking more questions, and broadening your experiences and your knowledge bank.

THE CRAFT ADVANTAGE

I think that there are four avenues to achieve the goal of learning everything:

1. **Read.** Read everything. Read nonprofessional work, fiction, nonfiction, and trade magazines. Connect outside of your normal sphere of interests; it will increase your creative thinking.

2. **Engage.** Ask questions of the subcontractors in the field, pay attention to your surroundings, and look for details that can inform the surroundings. Develop the skill to ask questions and listen.

3. **Experience.** Build something; try something completely new; start a new hobby; have many hobbies; travel with an eye on "seeing," not just visiting; take long walks in new places to think about the new place and about its relevance to other places. Store the knowledge.

4. **Think.** Practice positive and critical thinking. Look for the positive, look for the negative, look for the solutions, and look for the overall betterment. This perspective will fill your brain with massive knowledge that will help you and your team find solutions to many design challenges and increase joy in everything thing you do.

Perforated Silos: Learn What Matters to Others

Reach through your silo to other design and building partner silos of knowledge and experience. Invite everyone into your silo. The opposite of perforated silos are the typical closed, solid, uninviting silos that make up much of our design profession—not only in architecture but also in the design and business departments of many industries. None of this is really surprising or wrong except when a silo becomes fortified and then the solid silo can diminish learning and the formation of new ideas. The tribal nature of silos can allow for the development of an incredible level of expert skill, but it also can provide for stagnation and an "us-versus-them" culture that limits overall excellence.

My idea of a perforated-silo culture is less important in certain narrowly focused areas of research and industry. But in the architecture, engineering, and build culture, I think it is an imperative to have perforated silos because, quite simply, our actions impact the daily lives of the people who live in and around our design and build decisions. The increased transfer of knowledge between silos can help make the ideas better.

The more connected we are, the more comfortable we are to share across our silos of expertise, the more we feel invited to enter another silo, and the better chance we will have for a better built environment. Perforated silos can offer cost-effectiveness through fewer mistakes and a better experience for our clients. We have a better chance of achieving sustainable architecture, a more universally and accessible built environment, more equitable design solutions, and a lasting and growing positive experience for the people who engage in the built environment, which is just about everyone.

I see four tactics to perforate silos:

1. **Invite others in to share what you know.** Sharing what you know will help you know yourself better, which allows for improvement and allows others to see what you know so that they can learn. This will add more holes into the walls of the silos.

2. **Promote cross-training relationships with other silos.** Once the introductions have been made, foster a continuing relationship by creating cross-training opportunities. This will add more holes to the silos, and more people will reach through to engage and learn.

3. **Resist internal silos, and mix up your teams if needed.** What happens internally becomes an external attitude. Break down an internal silo culture so that you can have external relationships and more holes in your silo.

4. **Celebrate.** Celebrate the new knowledge, trust, and relationships developed from tactics 1, 2, and 3. This will ensure that the silos remain perforated and that positive engagement and growth continue.

Humans have always gathered in like-minded groups for a sense of security, comfort, and protection. Perforated silos is about reaching beyond and through to gain security, comfort, protection, longevity, and growth through engagement and trust from others.

Engage in and Complete the "Circle"

Don't live at your desk, don't stay in your studio … leave, go to the site. Spend many hours at the site—so much time that you become a fixture available to answer questions and, more importantly, to build relationships with the people who are interpreting your design and drawings and transforming them into a physical thing. Visit the projects after they are built and see how the building is being experienced.

The "circle" is composed of three segments: (1) the design, (2) the build, and (3) the experience. To complete the circle means to significantly engage with all three segments:

1 **The design.** The design team needs to see their design expertise realized in the field.

2 **The build.** The build team needs to see a design team that cares about the reality of construction.

3 **The experience.** The owner and users of the building need to see an architect that cares to see the good outcome and is willing to learn about the poor outcomes to never repeat.

The enemies of completing the circle are as follows:

1 **Poor training and the lack of desire to learn.** This includes architects/designers that don't care about, are uninterested in, and don't want to spend the time putting in the extra effort to be better.

2 **Profit erosion.** When a firm has poorly managed a project, the fee to be in the field is reduced or nonextant, meaning that each trip that the architect bills to the project is coming from profits; it doesn't come from the project fee, nor is it billable to the client. In these situations, the team members who want to visit the project under construction will hear from the project manager, "We don't have the fee." Ignore this and go on your own time. Your knowledge is your responsibility.

3 **Time.** When the design team is in a constant fire drill to get work done, the opportunity and desire to see the project under construction are dramatically reduced. Well-managed time is necessary to complete the circle.

These three enemies can be beat if the desire to learn is greater than any inconvenience- or status quo–driven barriers. Unfortunately, many professionals are lazy. I have seen it many a time: architects eating lunch at their desks and checking on their fantasy football teams instead of walking eight minutes to a job site near the office of a very significant and complex project. This was not a single person or a one-time observation; it was for the whole project, even with my prodding. One reason why the profession is in decline is because professionals are not feeling the urgency to perfect their craft. If they did, no one would need to prod or say, "Hey, go to the site. You will learn things." Rather, they would already be there soaking up the information.

Complete the circle on your own. You don't need fees, permission, or extra time—just go. It is your career and craft. The better you get at your craft, the more influence you will have to make projects better and the more confidence and ability you will have to mentor others.

Detail Excellence = Whole-Building Excellence

Buildings are often all about the connections, and when the connections are beautiful, thorough, and resolved, our construction partners can be more effective, the building will be more beautiful, and the maintenance life of the building can be improved, saving the client money and time. But detail excellence is not only about the connections; it is about the detailed thoroughness of the overall integrated design solution.

I think detail excellence falls into three categories:

1 **Searching for the best connections between components and materials.** Effective connection details will arise from a clear understanding and appreciation of the components and materials to be connected. Take a deep dive into the component and material characteristics to ensure that the connections are in harmony with the intended design goal. Each detail has an intended goal, like weatherproofing at a skylight, dampproofing at

the foundation/retaining walls, light transmission and reflectivity, acoustic separations, and so on. In our industry, we have many typical details that continue to get repeated because of past experience and dependability. Of course, how can this be bad? It really isn't, except for one thing: we stop exploring the best detail and settle on the good and proven detail. We need to take leadership on detail innovation to help push detail excellence and increase our value to our profession.

2 **System integration.** A building is a machine. It has internal moving parts and an exterior wrapper. It has an intended purpose and expected performance outcome. Unfortunately, some architects see the systems as separate activities that are essentially the background to the main performance of the building: aesthetics and experience. When the architect values the system integration as much as they value the aesthetics and experience, they can maximize the overall quality of the building and experience. The building can save more energy, be easier to maintain, and look great. Through intense system integration, the architect can help maximize the design budget to maximize quality and experience. If the architect is unaware or indifferent, they can miss opportunities to maximize quality and apply resources into more effective areas of a project design.

3. **Program optimization.** Details also live in how people use a building. Are they walking farther than needed to get to a critical system or function? Does the building design waste time and resources? Are the building spaces supporting the detail of operation? In the end, does the building make the lives of the people using it happier, easier, and more effective? Program optimization means taking a deep dive into how a building will be used and creating a design optimized around this understanding.

The whole-building thinker reaches for a whole-building understanding. They reach beyond their expertise and preconceived notions to try to develop a new understanding of what can make a particular detail, function, and program optimized to increase the overall quality and longevity of the project and experience.

Enhanced Communication and Coordination

Communication and coordination cross all aspects of the project are essential for a whole-building thinker. Enhanced communication and coordination means that they are conducted at a very proactive and an almost obsessive level of reinforcement, follow-up, and accuracy. Aside from the internal design coordination, there are two primary external environments of communication and coordination where skill is required: working with construction and working with your client.

External: Working with Construction

Invite yourself to pull-planning/subcontractor coordination schedule meetings. Most quality contractors want you there for the following five reasons:

1. It makes the architect more accountable for the delivery of the project when the architect can see the same picture that the contractor is seeing.

2. It helps the contractor to recruit the architect to address design and build issues.

3. It saves time in getting requests for information (RFIs) answered and reviewing a submittal when the architect is aware of the schedule pressures and is a participant in the schedule development.

4. It allows the contractor to shift some risk away from the build team and to the design team.

5. It is more fun, and it reduces stress by being a unified team versus a team at odds with one another.

Contractors who don't want the architect present may have something to hide and want the straightest line to the delivery of the project. They don't want any input that may alter the straight line even if is better for the quality of the project and team relationship. This is a red flag.

A whole-building contractor is just as important as a whole-building architect. Encourage and advise your clients to pick the whole-building contractor; it will make the communication and coordination of the project enjoyable and more effective.

External: Working with Your Client

Your client is often feeling much more stress than they let on. They are responsible for the money, the schedule, and the quality in a way that neither the architect nor the contractor can fully appreciate. A great project delivered, and the owners are heroes; a bad project, and they can suffer financially and hurt their career, reputation, and respect. It is all on them while having limited control. Clients often don't know the details of the process to design and build a project. They have to completely trust the team to know the details and to follow through with quality. What this means is that the architect needs to make it a personal mission to ensure that the client is fully apprised of and updated on the positive progress and not the messy nature of the process. Our job, with the builder, is to make a great meal in the kitchen for the client to enjoy in the dining room. The client should not see the messes and stresses and the potential drama associated with problem-solving unless they want to. The goal with enhanced communication and coordination is to make everyone's lives easier, especially your clients'.

"Design is not making beauty, beauty emerges from selection, affinities, integration, love."

LOUIS KAHN, ARCHITECT

THE SKILLS

INTELLIGENT IDEA INTEGRATION (GROWING INFLUENCE)

The message of this quote is straightforward: in a nutshell, real beauty comes from thoughtful action. It doesn't emerge from external contrivances; it emerges from the quality of integrated action. Intelligent idea integration requires a wide gaze to achieve beauty. In order to integrate all of the possible variables into something beautiful, the architect must embrace the whole-design challenge. It requires schools to teach from a whole-building perspective and architects, in practice, to mentor and embrace all aspects of the building, not just what can get published. It requires teaching critical thought and creativity in the pursuit of great ideas that make solutions easier and more effective. It requires teaching vision beyond the immediate need and seeking the best idea while not losing sight of the challenge at hand.

Intelligent idea integration is the second craft skill required to reverse the decline. It is made up of the five following topics:

1. Infinite Ideas: The Design Superpower
2. Concept, Brand, and Story
3. Horizon Seeking
4. Success Empathy
5. The Integration State of Mind

Infinite Ideas: The Design Superpower

Ideas drive solutions. Ideas flourish when there is a feeling of freedom to exchange and share ideas. When the environment feels selective and judgmental, ideas diminish and the possibilities for the better solution fade within the selective and judgmental context.

My infinite-ideas principle is this: Practice releasing yourself from one idea. Practice detaching yourself from your favorite idea. Practice creating multiple ideas without bias toward one or the other idea. Develop an attitude that allows others to feel that there are infinite ideas and that all ideas are welcome. Practice removing any subconscious secret agendas that sway the team toward a particular idea. Use facts, pros/cons, and persuasive arguments based in reason to inform the benefits and weaknesses of each option.

This requires the architect to deeply understand the ideas, apply critical thought, consider all aspects of the idea, consider the whole-building impacts of the ideas, and be able to present the vision of how a particular idea will impact the project/campus in the future.

The infinite-ideas approach only works with a sincere interest in finding the best idea, not just your idea because you want it. Your idea may be the best, and in most cases, after open dialogue and education about the ideas, your idea will be the chosen idea—but it may not be. If the approach has been sincere and objective, then you will be (or should be) happy no matter what idea was chosen.

The unfortunate reality about the architecture culture is that some architects can feel adversely judged by their colleagues when not creating visionary solutions, "publish-worthy" solutions, and cutting-edge innovations. This pressure often starts in school with teaching idol worship of famous architects and overemphasizing published work. This can extend outside of school through professional organizations doing the same thing. This is not necessarily wrong, because it helps learning and is fun and inspiring, but it is also easier than focusing on the harder subjects and process to make the most of more average yet important buildings. My point is that our complicated culture of design education, emotion, and motivations can bias some architects against an objective, infinite-ideas approach and sway them toward an emotional approach that can alienate our clients and industry partners. Infinite ideas means that you have ultimate confidence in your ability to generate ideas. When you have this confidence, you fear no idea. You are empowered to maximize the best for the team, and your team is empowered to share ideas. In the end, the best idea wins, the built environment wins, and the relationships positively grow as you look forward to the next project.

> Think of infinite ideas as a design superpower making all things possible. The more of us that practice this superpower, the quicker the decline curve is reversed and the more our influence grows. Intelligent idea integration depends on infinite ideas to ensure that the best idea is the most intelligent idea for that project and client.

Concept, Brand, and Story

Intelligent idea integration requires an understanding of the importance of the concept, brand, and story behind existing projects and proposed ideas for new projects.

All projects have some concept, brand, and story that are driving decisions. In some cases, the concepts may have been bad or minimal enough to have no real impact. In other cases, the concepts existed, but no one on the team championed the ideas throughout the project to ensure that they were realized. Establishing the concept, brand, and story for a project is a very hard task. It is even harder to maintain the vision throughout the project. As a project progresses, other real pressures, such as cost, schedule, procurement, municipality and entitlement challenges, and so on, can shift attention away from the original ideas and goals for the project.

INTELLIGENT IDEA INTEGRATION

It is the architect's job to establish the concept, brand, and story; build consensus through an infinite-ideas approach; and champion that approach through to the very end of the project.

Concept, brand, and story are important for the following reasons:

1. It unifies the team to maximize effective decision-making.

2. It amplifies the design by disciplining the design process to reinforce the concept, brand, and story.

3. It creates an elevator speech to help convey the project design intention to various stakeholders within an organization. Projects that can be described simply have a better chance of getting necessary approvals, surviving budget cuts, and having a consensus of support to navigate any unforeseen challenges.

4. An established concept, brand, and story can become the foundation for any marketing plan, articles, and interviews.

THE CRAFT ADVANTAGE

Not all projects benefit the same way. Higher-profile projects will benefit the most, but it is also necessary for lower-profile projects to ensure a more disciplined design process. I define the concept, brand, and story as follows:

1. **The concept** is the unified design idea that accommodates the current project program, cost, and design needs, as well as the vision and any future growth and campus integration as needed.

2. **The brand** is a sentence and graphic that represent the concept. Think like a product advertiser using a single line of text supported by a simple yet powerful graphic to place the brand into the brain of the viewer. Do the same for the project.

3. **The story** is the background narrative that supports the concept and brand and describes why the project even exists. Once the story is told, the concept and brand just make sense.

> **When all three align, the design will resonate with success and promote intelligent idea integration.**

Horizon Seeking

Horizon seeking is the ability to see beyond the immediate needs and perspective. It is about trying to see around corners, and it is essential for effective intelligent idea integration. The ideas that are aligned with the "horizon" are the ideas that often bring in more work and can anticipate potential challenges that may limit more opportunities for idea integration. Horizon seeking is about seeking trends that can benefit your practice, the profession, and the client while also seeking any potential pitfalls.

I love patterns, and I think of trends as unique patterns that can emerge within a market, an industry, a profession, and a culture. I focus on three primary areas of horizon seeking:

1 **Market/industry trends.** Trends are driven by a competitive marketplace requiring accelerated delivery of projects to save time, construction costs, new building types, amenities, unique design solutions, new building systems, and so on. This is obvious, of course, but as architects, we are expected to know more than others. Clients expect the architect within a specific industry to be able to intelligently discuss industry trends, be current with trends, and be able to describe how they may effect the needs of the client. When an architect can't do this, they no longer look like experts and can lose value in the eyes of the client. Clients are looking for guidance from experts and not a drafting service. It is essential that architects seek knowledge and be experts within their specialty.

2. **Client needs aligned with future trends.** This area of horizon seeking is a very important way to win new work (I describe this further in the Skills to Shape section of this book). It starts with the architect overlaying a trend onto their client's need to stay competitive, provide new services to their customers/residents, and be ready for the future. If the architect has been paying attention to the trends and also paying attention to their client, they can propose ideas that can turn into future projects. They can help their client with visioning and be an essential ingredient in the future growth and success of the client. The client's success can become the architect's success.

3. **Horizon planning and protection.** The straw view, as I described earlier, is the worst enemy of seeking the horizon and anticipating change that can hurt or help a practice or a client. The limited aperture of the straw view may be comforting to some by reducing the amount of information and potential distraction, but in the end, it can reduce any positive impact by not allowing the architect to consider all of the information available and potentially destroying a practice. "Eyes wide open" is the best policy for architects.

Practice the skill of looking outward past the immediate needs, past the immediate worries, and past the immediate distractions. Look far outward, and learn what you can to push your vision forward. Think hard, research, and seek diverse ideas and knowledge to help you see further and further.

> **The essence of intelligent idea integration is knowledge integrated with a forward-looking vision.**

Success Empathy

Success empathy is empathy in practice. It is about sincerely seeking information to maximize the quality of a design solution, tune an idea specifically to your client's needs, and make the final product the most enjoyable for the people using the building. Have you ever had a conversation with someone and you can tell that, while they may be smiling or nodding their head, they are not listening? Well, this is an experience that people have had with some architects. Some architects can be so busy thinking of what they want that they are not always very good listeners and, as a result, not very good at reading body language and hearing the information that is in between the lines of what is being said. It is often in between the lines where the best information lies. Success empathy exists in this zone.

Success empathy is my idea to retool our design perception and information gathering toward the emotions that are often driving the many decisions about, reactions to, attitudes about, and goals behind a need. Success empathy requires us to develop our skills to read what is between the lines better and understand the emotions that can help improve the design solutions. The purpose is to be more effective in winning work, winning interviews, losing work to your advantage, designing projects, tuning a design to the various user groups, and having long-lasting relationships with our industry partners.

The following is a high-level summary of the steps for incorporating success empathy into a design and information-gathering process. I will be expanding this system in the future. The success empathy process is flexible, so it can be adapted to the client's rules of engagement with their teams. Even if access is limited, the process can still be successful with the leaders.

1. **Remove your own preconceived notions.** Make no assumptions about how a particular user group will use a space and what they may need. Remove any preconceived notions about people. Be open to all personality types, and find joy in the wide variety of people and jobs.

2. **Have discussions first before having meetings.** No conference rooms—at first. Conference rooms set up a more formal expectation of engagement, which can reduce interaction. You want a casual and relaxed place for the first few meetings. Find out what is the client's idea for project success. Have conversations with the client leaders and user group leaders. Ideally these

conversations are one-on-one or in small groups. The purpose is not only to get to know each other but also to learn their personalities and what they like the most about the existing building or goals for the future building.

3 **Listen as if you are doing their job.** Learn like you are responsible for making everyone's jobs easier and more effective. Apply what you have learned. Follow up, as required, to refine and test the ideas.

4 **Ask questions and propose improvement ideas.** Think of this process as a casual and swirling helix of questions, answers, and ideas as you move through the conversation. Always have a dedicated note taker while you facilitate the conversation. Your focus must be unwavering to be effective.

Success empathy is the beginning of a very powerful process in development that can enrich intelligent idea integration and retool how architects program and design a building.

The Integration State of Mind

The ultimate gain from intelligent idea integration is a state of mind that seeks an integration that can harmonize and resonate with a design solution and design relationships to near perfection. This may seem lofty, for sure, but I think it is possible for our profession to approach a level of expertise and profound impact that will ensure that our influence grows and that we are effective in improving the profession and the built environment. With an integration state of mind, we can become essential, without question.

The integration state of mind is an attitude that projects optimism in whatever is encountered. It is based in happiness and the joy of realizing ideas. It is an attitude that embraces challenges and conflicts as opportunities to be better as a team and to find the best solutions for the client. It is an arms-wide-open, eyes-wide-open approach to problem-solving.

Below are the steps to an integration state of mind:

1. **You can't integrate what you don't know.** Your consultant team is no different. They can't optimize a solution that considers other parts of the information if they don't know the information. It is the architect's job to inform the team and lead with a perspective that considers all discipline information.

2. **Embrace your design and construction partners' risks.** Learn their risks, learn what keeps them up at night, and truly care. Ask questions.

INTELLIGENT IDEA INTEGRATION

3 **Reduce risks by sharing the risks.** When does any team or project benefit when partners of the team are overburdened with risk and stress? Never. Reduce the risk by helping. Have discussions to find a way to address and fill any gaps to reduce the pressure. I know this may seem like a strange idea to some, but perforated silos is about reaching from one discipline silo into another discipline silo to learn, engage, share, and improve. Imagine what can be achieved if we truly act as a team. It starts with sharing risk.

4 **Fill gaps.** The goal is a fully integrated design and an optimal solution for the client. This can only happen if we take responsibility for filling coordination gaps. If you see a gap, mention it, offer help, and make it a priority to ensure that it is filled.

5 **Lead with joy and laughter.** No team is perfect, no project is ideal, and every team and individual has pressures that they do not share. Always assume the best, be empathetic, and lead with optimism.

When intelligent idea integration is practiced with an integration state of mind, teams will be more effective, craft will be optimized, relationships will grow, decline will be reversed, and our influence will be essential to our clients.

> Over time, the built environment—wherever architects practice—will be improved.

"Better than a thousand days of diligent study is one day with a great mentor."

JAPANESE PROVERB

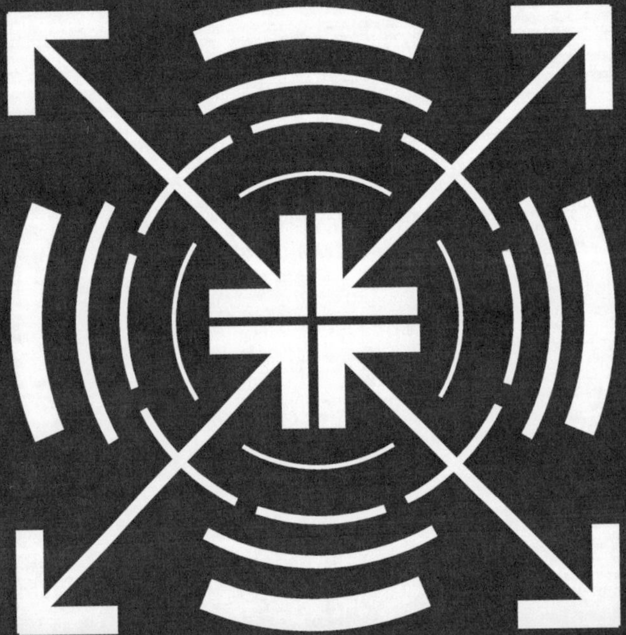

THE SKILLS

ACCOUNTABILITY AND MENTORSHIP (FOLLOW-THROUGH AND GROWTH)

Without a culture of accountability and mentorship, we will never improve. The past generations of architecture had a culture with an open environment of critical judgment with a dose (or sometimes a bucket) of shame thrown in to make the point that the work quality needed to improve. This was not a great way to mentor, but it did motivate higher-quality work and becoming better at learning the craft. Going forward, architects need to develop the skill to communicate accountability without using shame as one of the ingredients to motivate. Instead, mentor by promoting the importance of craft and skill excellence for an improved built environment. Motivate the young architects to be in the field and to partner with the construction team in realizing the project. Convey through engagement the joy of excellence and the beauty that can be realized. This kind of leadership will make accountability and mentorship values that are practiced and passed down to future architects.

Accountability and mentorship is the last fundamental craft skill required to reverse the decline.

It is made up of the five following topics:

1. Professional Accountability
2. Personal Accountability
3. Practice Accountability
4. Mentorship
5. Volunteering and Community

Professional Accountability

Professional accountability is when an architect considers the impact of their decisions on the profession as a whole and not just their immediate needs for their practice or personal goals.

The challenge with being accountable to the profession is that an architect needs to be prepared to be selfless in their decision-making. The prospect of this can be considered a fantasy when applied within the reality of architecture in practice, but it is a necessary fantasy to turn it into a reality.

Here is a common scenario: An architect needs a project to keep up with payroll. They have been asked to respond to a Request for Proposal (RFP) by a potential client. The architect knows that if they can make their fee very low, they stand a great chance of getting the project. So, they undercut their competitors and win the project. They are successful in bringing in more revenue, albeit low revenue, to keep their practice open while at the same time lowering the fee standard for other architects going forward. The architect has hurt the profession. They don't mean to; they are just trying to survive until the next project.

This situation is so real and common that it is hard to hold it against the architect. Many architects are doing it to some degree, and because all architects are playing with their fee to win instead of holding a standard, the standard is "whatever wins" and not what is best for the profession.

How can a standard be upheld when there is no standard to reference except what clients will pay and how low an architect will go? The good news for clients is that with each passing day, architect fees are going lower and lower because of the previous scenario. Over time, this situation can be reversed if we take the following actions:

1. **Create a national fee schedule.** Architects should work with the American Institute of Architects (AIA) to create a national fee schedule for the different project types in our profession. This idea has been discussed but never seems to become real. The fee schedule would be based on a fee range, the scale of the project, complexity, and regional location. This would allow architects to be able to point to a standard as a datum to justify their fee. It would allow all architects to know when they are proposing a fee below the national fee schedule and if they are undercutting the market and hurting the profession. Maybe, when a client sees this in comparison to other architect fees, it may trigger questions about the low fee and if the scope of services is the same compared to the competitors who are holding the standard. This scrutiny may help to motivate architects to stay within the fee range.

2. **Protect the profession through good business management.** Poor business management can make the architect vulnerable to having to compromise the standard to stay alive. Plan, save, and lead. Professional accountability, realized as a team over time, will create higher fees across the board.

Personal Accountability

In my view, personal accountability in architecture is made up of five primary goals:

1. **Never stop learning.** Growth is life. When a person has an optimistic attitude, they will be able to grow with the pressures of the practice. The more a person knows, the more they can adapt with the least amount of stress. This can include formal and informal continuing education and reading: reading about your industry and outside of your industry. It means attending conferences to broaden your perspective, having conversations with your industry partners to learn what they are learning. In the end, the more you know, the better you will be at leading yourself and your practice.

2. **Stay healthy and don't drink ... or, at least, minimize consumption.** There has been an ongoing joke about architects being alcoholics because of being misunderstood, tortured geniuses that are never satisfied with the final product. While it is true that architects tend to see more imperfections in the final work than others see, there is no excuse for reinforcing the stereotype by hammering your personal health. Our profession is very hard, and it is very stressful. While other professions have many stresses, what makes

ACCOUNTABILITY AND MENTORSHIP

architecture unique is the very wide spectrum of responsibilities—ranging from the art, to the science, to the building of an idea—while trying to make money and reinforce our value in a world where many think they can do architecture because they have a new "design-your-own-building" app. Stay healthy so that you can keep fighting for a better profession.

3 **Stay healthy and exercise ... or, at least, take walks.** Walking is the best for thinking, and we are in a "thinking" profession. Walks help us to create better ideas, sort through challenges, be better at problem-solving, and be creative. Stay healthy by walking. Movement is life.

4 **Work hard and work happy.** Optimism combined with hard work is the energy that drives success for you and your team. When your team sees your optimism, they become optimistic and enjoy the challenging work instead of dreading it.

5 **Hold a high standard of what is right based on reason.** Be clear, moral, ethical, and honest. Speak truth with respect; be strong in the face of weakness and corrupt thinking. Architecture, to me, is one of the most important human endeavors that impacts the daily lives of people. Our work can make life better or worse. Because of this, we have a heightened responsibility to hold high standards of behavior and high-quality design decisions. Our design choices need to be tested with the following question: "Does this design make life better for the people who will use this building?" If the answer is "no," then change the design. If others don't want to change, be persuasive and present alternatives.

> Personal accountability is personal, for sure, but all high standards start with the individual and project outward to the profession and to the practice of architecture.

Practice Accountability

Practice accountability is when an architect applies professional and personal accountability to their daily practice of architecture.

Practice accountability is made up of the following categories:

1. **Real-time mentoring.** This is mentoring that occurs throughout the workday as you work with your team. Instead of directing a team member to do something, real-time mentoring is when you take the time to explain why it needs to be done. When a young professional has the context behind the work, they learn quicker and become invested in the quality of the final product. They become owners of the activity. Take the time to share the stories behind the issues and provide sidebars with less-related context to help broaden their perspective. In the end, they will become better professionals and you will have more time.

2. **Teach.** Transfer wisdom. You may not think so, but any practicing architect has learned a great deal that can benefit the team members in the practice and students in the university. Teach to be a better professional: what

we teach, we get better at understanding, and others benefit from the knowledge. We only know what we know when we know it. Learning is a very personal process, but it starts with someone wanting to share what they have learned for the betterment of other people.

3. **Reinforce quality.** Don't let bad quality slide because of being busy or for fear of hurting someone's feelings. When you hide the truth from a person, you are showing them great disrespect. People tend to ignore bad quality because they don't want to have the stress of confrontation. Most sincere professionals want to get better, and honest input respectfully delivered is almost always appreciated even though it may be difficult at first. If constructive input is ignored, then that team member is probably not a good fit within a quality-centric practice.

4. **Promote career growth.** We are all on our own adventure in our career. You need to focus on helping your team members achieve their career goals. This will help your practice be more successful, and it will increase staff retention. It is the nature of most architects to strive to get better and better. If your practice celebrates this, you will have happier and higher-performing team members.

> Professional, personal, and practice accountability, applied consistently and with passion and precision, will, over time, dramatically improve our profession as a whole and help to reverse the decline into greater influence.

Mentorship

Mentorship, as a value practiced daily, is the best way to grow quality over time. It is strange to me that mentoring is not more consistently applied in our profession. I have experienced firms that institute formal mentoring programs because mentoring wasn't happening. These programs are initiated not because of the greater good of transferring wisdom but as a device to increase employee retention. At least mentorship is happening, but because it is forced or "encouraged," it doesn't have the same impact as when the person does it as a value to improve another person's knowledge and skill and the profession. Promote mentoring as an everyday value.

In addition to real-time mentoring needed for effective practice accountability, the following are some techniques for improved mentoring:

1. **Ride along.** Invite your team members to ride with you to a site visit or meetings. Use the time to share knowledge, prep them for the meeting, and establish context, where needed, to understand the information. Use the time to check on how they are doing and new happenings in their life.

2. **Site visits with the team.** Take the time to tour the team or an individual on a project site visit. Point out everything that you can. Stop and discuss details. Have discussions with the superintendent and subcontractors when appropriate.

ACCOUNTABILITY AND MENTORSHIP

3. **Give immediate feedback.** When you notice an area that needs to be improved—whether it was performance in a meeting, the quality of work, or a discussion with others—don't wait to give feedback at some yearly review. Pull the person aside as soon as possible and discuss improvement. This tactic helps everyone. Instead of letting poor quality or an area of improvement slide without comment while suffering quietly, get into the habit of providing immediate feedback. It will help the staff member get better more quickly and reduce your own stress. Courage and clarity are rewarded by having a higher-performing team. Don't fear confrontation. Embrace the opportunity for improvement.

4. **Own a meeting.** Have a team member own a meeting to learn how to run a meeting.

5. **Opportunities to present.** Junior staff members don't get many opportunities, if any, to present after they leave school. Make opportunities for them.

6. **Teach to mentor others.** Set up a team culture that promotes mentoring at all levels of the organization. Everyone has something to teach. The more knowledge sharing there is, the better the teamwork, relationships, and growth will be.

Think of mentoring as your investment in your growth, your team's growth, and a better profession.

Volunteering and Community

Architecture is directly connected to community. The community is living and working in our buildings. An architect who doesn't engage in the community is an architect with blinders on, who is missing the opportunity to learn, win more work, and contribute to the community that we serve.

The following are ways to engage in volunteering and community:

1. **Teach in youth STEM programs.** Volunteer in elementary school STEM programs. Many of these schools and programs are looking for professionals to help broaden their curriculum. Take advantage of this opportunity to help teach architecture and related subjects, like bridge design, understanding the built environment, working on design and build teams, and collaboration skills for a successful built environment.

2. **Teach at a university.** Volunteer or get a part-time adjunct professor job at a university. These students are getting ready to enter the profession, so your input and knowledge will help their transition greatly and make them more effective partners in the profession. Make the time to teach. The benefits are massive for the school, the students, and the profession. As a side benefit, you are able to find potential students to offer internships to or who you can guide to other architects looking for new team members.

ACCOUNTABILITY AND MENTORSHIP

3. **Volunteer in community organizations.** You can volunteer at churches, clubs, community gardens, museums, and so on. This has been a strategy many architecture practices have used to make sure that they have the best opportunities for more work. Many firms require all levels of staff to engage in the community. It is a win-win strategy that can benefit the practice and the community at the same time.

4. **Offer free work.** Offering free work can help build relationships and help the community organization understand the scope of what they need completed for their campus or organization. Free work is free work. It should never be offered with the contingency of winning the full project. Offer without strings attached. Offer because it is the right thing to do. Many community organizations have very little money, and the goodwill shown will help them define their design needs while reducing financial pressure and helping them better their situation.

These are all options that some architects engage in at a very high level, while others do nothing. Volunteering is a key requirement to successfully apply the Craft Advantage to reverse the decline.

> **The more that we engage with our community, the more opportunities and positive impact we can have to grow our craft and the more overall influence we will have for a better built environment and profession.**

"Skill is the unified force of experience, intellect, and passion in their operation."

JOHN RUSKIN, WRITER AND PHILOSOPHER

SKILLS TO SHAPE

Skill to Define	Skill to Lose
Skill to Start	Skill to Grow
Skill to Lead	Skill to Adjust
Skill for Introspection	Skill to Deliver
Skill to Understand	Skill to Breathe
Skill to Communicate	Skill to See
Skill to Win	Skill to Integrate

THE SKILLS

SKILLS TO SHAPE

I interpret Ruskin's quote in the following way: Skill takes time, hence you need experience and intellect to see what skill matters and the passion to apply the skill. Skill needs to be applied so that improvement through the operation, or use, of the skill can be achieved.

The following are skills to shape the mission, that I think are important to consider, that can help to unify and shape the team and extended relationships. They are the result of my experiences and, of course, don't represent all the skills needed. Use the following skills as high-level fundamentals to define your style. In the end, the goal is to shape the mission, be effective, and be centered in trust with respect to our team, industry partners, and clients. While the following may be useful, you will need to adjust and refine, as required, according to your unique context and goals.

At the end of the day, I think the following:

> **Craft is skill applied with passion and precision.**

Simply put, any skill requires practice, but you can't practice what you don't know.

Skill to Define
What Is Design?

Many architects can't answer the question "what is design?" Yet many proceed into a process that they can't define or understand. For us to be excellent in our craft, we need to strive to be experts at understanding our craft of design and at least be able to have a definition for it.

Step 1: Discuss the Definition

Design is both a noun and verb: as a noun, it is a plan or drawing produced to show the look and function of something, and as a verb, it is the act of designing the noun. I decided that the common definition of design is not specific enough for what architects and other designers are actually doing, so I created my own definition to be used in practice. My definition of design, in practice, is based on determining the required decision points for a successful design. In my definition, decision points are the particular characteristics, goals, attributes, and functions that the design needs to have to be effective. My definition is as follows:

> **Design is the act of prioritizing decision points within a set of constraints into an integrated and effective whole that is aligned with a vision and an expectation of performance.**

Design is the act of prioritizing decision points into an integrated and effective whole.

Step 2: Discuss Who "Owns" the Design

Take a moment to discuss what design is with the team. This may seem like an unnecessary step in a compacted project schedule or not desired by the designers who don't want to collaborate and let people into the kitchen, but with the door more open, the accountability for the design will increase and overall quality can increase.

The question: Who are the designers?

The answer: Everyone.

The discussion point: While designers are "everyone," most people don't think that they design, so the designer activity becomes siloed and specialized. When design is siloed, the responsibility for design is siloed. When responsibility for design is siloed, quality can drop because of less exposure to and interaction with other points of view. Design quality can increase when the responsibility for quality is owned by everyone. Design decision points can be anything that can impact the design; that means that everyone has, or many people have, some influence on the design decision points. When architects embrace this notion and have the confidence of infinite ideas described in the Intelligent Idea Integration section, their designs will be better, be more effective, and have many more people in support of the solutions, which will increase the number of relationships and project opportunities.

Skill to Start
The Ten Design Decision Points Before Starting to Design

Design is a process that is dependent on quality information before starting to design. This also includes setting the "design table" for an effective design experience. Many architects jump right into designing the solution without having taken the time to design the relationships and the context for a positive experience prior to digging into the design process. This is like planting a garden without first knowing how deep the roots need to be, the required nutrition and sun exposure, and the optimal size. If you follow this process, you end up starting over and wasting time.

The following are the ten design decision points before starting to design. Implement where you can to ensure the best overall project experience. If you engage early, you can design much of the overall project framework.

1. **Research and establish the big vision that is aligned with the goals of the owner.** Use the idea to unify the direction of the project. This is not a list of aesthetic qualities; it is a unifying goal that will be refined during the concept design phase, but before designing, it will help direct the project goals.

2. **Pick your contractor.** Your direct partner in the project is the contractor, so do what you can to influence the choice. Pick a contractor that shares your values and embraces collaboration and transparency.

3. **Pick your team.** "'A' players only" should be your hiring goal. They make everyone's lives easier.

4. **Pick your client.** Work with clients that share your values and will embrace collaboration and transparency. Don't accept a client that will make the experience unpleasant. Say "no." An unpleasant client will cause stress and drama that will affect the team's performance and impact other projects in the practice. In the end, you will probably lose money, the delivery will not be at the highest level, and you will open yourself up to criticism that can hurt your reputation for future work.

5. **Design the consultant team.** Use only trusted design partners. Their effectiveness becomes your effectiveness.

6. **Design the schedule.** Establish the design schedule very quickly and use it to help the contractor design the overall project schedule. This way, you can protect the design durations. The schedule drives the project, so if the schedule is not designed properly, there will be many stressful moments.

7. **Design the project delivery.** Pick the delivery based on your highest chance of design collaboration. The lowest collaboration model is design-bid-build, the most restrictive is design-build, and the most collaborative is Construction Manager at Risk. These are discussed in more detail in the section Skill to Deliver: DBB, CMaR, or DB.

8 **Design the "buckets" for the project budget.** This is where moving quickly is very important. Establish a design budget framework very quickly to integrate into the contractor's overall project budget. The earlier that this is done, the more likely it will be that the important design elements represented in the budget. Reality lies within the budget. The budget starts to stratify into varying priorities very quickly.

9 **Design the project communication and delivery for speed and quality.**

10 **Embrace all resources to achieve project goals.** This means people, tools, and processes.

Skill to Hire
Who to Hire

The most important design decision you can make is hiring the right people. You should strive to hire "A" players only, and they should embrace your practice values. This list is what I consider whenever hiring a new team member.

Love Building

Design Integration

Have Vision

Respect Budgets

Respect Schedules

Build Relationships

Quality of Craft

Joyous

Skill to Lead
Team Alignment

After you have hired your "A" players and assembled what you hope is a high-performing team, the next step is to align your team with expectations that drive high performance. Team alignment is driven by open conversation to remove doubts, define roles, discuss conflicts, role-play scenarios, and organize the communication process of the team.

The following is a list of topics to consider in your conversations with the team:

1 **Make it engaging.** This is intended to be fun, personal, and nonwork related. It is for the team to get to know each other and break down any barriers. You should inspire through action, laughter, and joy in the conversation.

2 **Discuss schedules.** Have an open discussion about the project and personal schedules to help reduce stress and plan more effectively.

3 **Discuss roles.** This is a very important conversation that can have some stress, which is why many leaders don't have the conversation. They fear disappointment or conflict from the team members who may have a misunderstanding of their role on a project. Role clarity is critical for a team to be high performing. Don't evade establishing clarity about roles and responsibilities.

4. **Discuss the leadership roles.** The bigger the team, the more important it is to establish the different tiers of roles and responsibilities. Don't soft-pedal who reports to whom or who is responsible for what. Clarity may be difficult for some, but it is a necessity for a team to be high performing.

5. **Discuss conflict.** Discuss how the team will handle conflict, disagreements between team members, or external challenges that may arise from the consultants, contractor, or client. Discuss and prepare.

6. **Diagram the team.** Have an organization chart. An org chart drives clarity and helps to remove ambiguity about roles and responsibilities.

Skill to Lead
Rules of Positive Engagement

Now that your team understands its roles and responsibilities and you have had any hard but necessary conversations with anyone on the team regarding misunderstandings of their role, you go to the next level and discuss the rules of engagement. These are rules of respect for one another and how you expect the team to interact going forward. This is easy when you have "A" players.

The following is a list of topics to consider in your conversation about positive engagement with the team:

SKILLS TO SHAPE

1. **Trust is earned, not deserved.** Building trust by earning trust means to build confidence with others by action and follow-through.

2. **Follow through.** The act of doing what you say that you are going to do is the key ingredient to building trust.

3. **Pursue excellence.** Pursuing excellence is a value that is essential to achieve high-quality craft.

4. **Open dialogue.** Don't keep secrets. Promote open discussion and dialogue to get the best solution and to allow everyone on the team to have an opportunity to contribute ideas to the process. Best idea wins.

5. **Responsibility is taken, not given.** "A" players, by their nature, take responsibility. You need to promote this culture so that the team members can grow their skills and further support the effectiveness and efficiency of the team. More people trying to fill any gaps will always help the project.

6. **Beware of vanity.** Vanity can be the troublemaker on a team. We all feel vanity poke at us in meetings when we feel like we are not being heard or being ignored. We feel it when we don't receive the level of credit that we expect. We can feel it when someone else gets promoted. Vanity is natural, but it needs to be managed by the person so that the team doesn't lose focus with emotional distractions or unnecessary conflicts. Hire only "A" players; they often are very secure in their view of themselves, so their vanity stays personal and does not become a distraction to the team.

TEAM ALIGNMENT

1. **Have a Conversation**
   Not project related, but personal stories

2. **Discuss Schedules**
   Availability, personal commitments, preferences

3. **Discuss Roles**
   Design, coordination, management, production

4. **Discuss the Leadership Roles**
   Review accountability and reporting

5. **Discuss Conflict**
   Role-play possible conflict scenarios

6. **Diagram the Team**
   Create an org chart and review with the team

RULES OF POSITIVE ENGAGEMENT

1 **Trust Is Earned, Not Deserved**
Build trust by earning trust

2 **Follow Through**
Say what you mean and do what you promise

3 **Pursue Excellence**
Balance time, quality, and relationships

4 **Open Dialogue**
Let ideas flow until the best idea wins

5 **Responsibility Is Taken, Not Given**
Fill gaps while respecting roles

6 **Beware of Vanity**
You shine brighter when you let others shine

Skill to Lead
Watch for the Signs of Team Dysfunction

High-performing teams and realizing projects are adventures in emotion and interaction. You will be able to tell how well the team is feeling by watching for high-functioning and dysfunctional behavior. The following is a list of the signs to watch for:

1. **Laughter vs. no laughter.** This is really simple: if the team is feeling good and the interaction is going well, there is laughter. Laughter is the best sign that all is well on the team. It is also contagious and helps keep the team morale up.

2. **Willing contribution vs. selective contribution.** When a person is distracted by vanity, their willingness to contribute may be reduced or be very selective. If that happens, reach out for a conversation. Don't wait.

3. **Open dialogue vs. defensive arguments.** Similar to sign 2, when the conversation is free-flowing without judgment or defensive arguments, all is well on the team. Once someone gets defensive, their vanity may be in play.

4. **On time vs. late.** Being on time shows respect to your team members; being late shows disrespect and a cavalier attitude toward the success of the team.

5. **No sarcasm vs. sarcasm.** Sarcasm has been referred to as the lowest form of wit. In the Greek language, it means "to tear." It also can be fun, and some have elevated the use of sarcasm to an art form. The bottom line is that sarcasm is not good for the team. Direct communication is the best path forward to ensure that productive and happy communication is happening on the team.

6 Fun vs. dread. Work is fun, and the team members can find joy in realizing a project with a great team. If a team becomes dysfunctional, the fun is replaced with dread—dread coming to work, dread listening to others speak, dread attending meetings and doing anything extra for the quality realization of the project. Inspire fun and joy by making sure that the team is in harmony.

HIGH-FUNCTIONING	DYSFUNCTIONAL
There is laughter	There is no laughter
Everyone contributes	Selective contributions
Open dialogue	Defensive arguments
Team members are on time	Team members are late
There is no sarcasm	There is sarcasm
The work is fun	Fun is replaced with dread

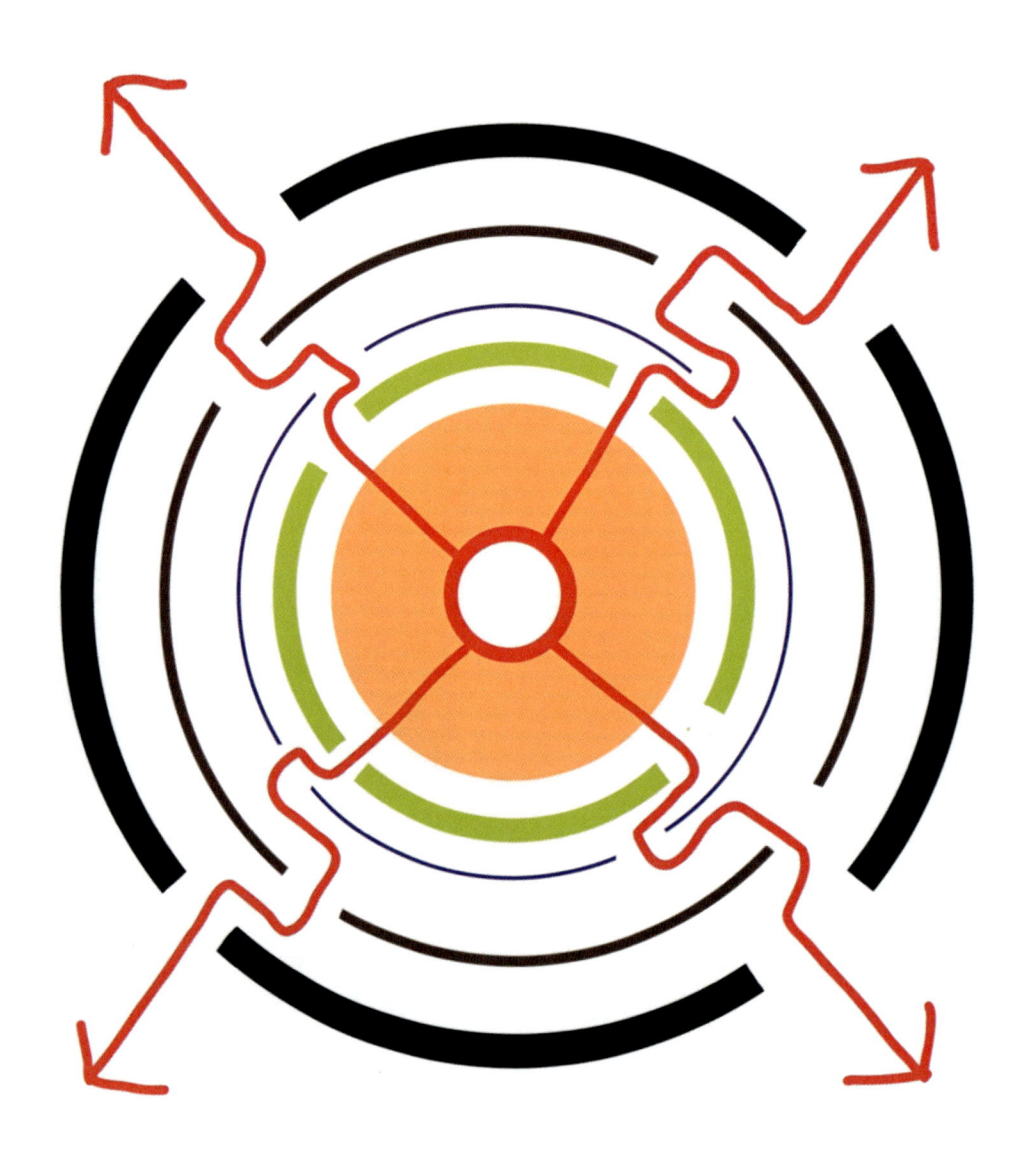

Architects Explained: Decoding Architects

Skill for Introspection
Architects Explained

It's a skill to be able to "know thyself"; when you do, you can improve. The following are some general facts about architects. There are many exceptions, and not everyone will agree with this list, but these characteristics are shared by many architects. My overarching point is that architects need to know ourselves first to better integrate with our industry partners who often experience our unique and eccentric characteristics.

It is unrealistic to think we can effectively integrate with other professionals and clients before, first, knowing ourselves. We need to have introspection into what drives us individually and collectively as a profession.

Architecture as a profession is very complex, often requiring very complex interactions to bring a project into reality and to build the lasting relationships for future projects. Our first design problem is an inward task that sets the table for the outward task of realizing an idea into a physical form with our construction partners and clients.

The following list is our first step to decoding how we think, our priorities, and our mission. It is the first step to realizing a better profession and, ultimately, a better built environment.

Characteristics That are Often Unique to Architects

1. Architects are generalists with detail skills (artists with inventor-science-detail minds).

2. Architects are pressure-cooked (trained) in an educational and professional environment of judgment.

3. Architects believe that architecture can save the world or, at least, make it better.

4. Architects can fear losing control of an idea.

5. Architects fear being judged by an idea that they lost control of, so they want contact with the idea throughout the project.

6. Some architects can be arrogant, entitled (but not mean-spirited), and driven by a desire to be recognized.

7. Architects are often trained with history, precedent, and "famous architect worship" first, then, second, with practical applications and science.

8. Architects can care greatly about building details that others don't see or care about—caring to the point of emotional wreckage.

9. Most architects are nonlinear thinkers and approach challenges in a nonlinear way.

10. Architects are trained to start solving a problem at a "30,000-foot" macro perspective.

11. Architects are trained to drill down to nauseating details that no one else may care about.

12. Architects can focus too much on the tree while missing the forest.

13 Architects can judge others who don't see the forest that they see.

14 Architects want to be respected by the builder, and they want to build.

15 Architects want the builder to have vision, care about a world view, and care about the built environment.

16 Architects are not initially educated with building skills, construction budgets, and the builder's risk.

17 Architects are not initially educated about project development, business financial constraints, and the developer's risk.

18 Architects are not trained for conflict. This skill is learned through conflict.

19 Architects leave school with little knowledge of the contractor's and developer's world and with little respect for the developer.

20 Architects are often resistant to asking for additional money for additional services rendered.

21 Architects tend to underestimate the value of their services and skills.

22 Architects are very smart and have a broad range of skills.

23 Architects value relationships and trust more than money and power.

24 Many architects love conversations about what is possible, especially with coffee, wine, and interesting people.

Skill for Introspection
How Architects Like to Work

Knowing thyself and having a specific idea of how you like to work is an important skill to elevate our craft, unity, and quality. You can't improve what you don't know, you can't request what you don't know, and you can't reinforce a value if you don't have specific thoughts about the value and what you require for the best project performance. The following are some general facts about how architects like to work. Again, there will be many exceptions, and not everyone will agree with the following list, but many of the insights and desires are shared by many architects.

Architects like ...

1. To be involved at the beginning of an idea.
2. To be part of a team to solve challenges and not be dictated to regarding what the solution should be.
3. To provide options to understand the challenges and build consensus on the best path forward.
4. To be involved in honest engagement and transparency between the disciplines.
5. To be recognized for our quality work.
6. To receive constructive criticism to improve.
7. To create beauty and cost value and the balance of both.

8 To be accountable for the coordination and delivery of a project.

9 To take calculated risks for the betterment of the project.

10 To work hard for the success of the overall team.

11 To have fun while working hard.

12 To hire team members that will improve the design experience.

13 To be asked for advice on site selections and design strategies.

14 To have follow-through opportunities after a project is complete.

15 To earn respect through excellent work. Respect earned instead of deserved.

16 To work with people who try to have an open and active mind to find solutions.

17 To work with honest contractors.

18 To work with honest developers.

19 To work with people who strive for quality, not just the easy and cheapest solution.

20 To work with owners that love and respect their employees.

21 To work with employees who feel empowered by their organization to find good solutions.

22 To help support and realize a building with the contractor and to be included in the process.

When an architect strives to know themselves and have a clear understanding of how they like to work, combined with the courage to convey and champion their preferences, then the next level of craft can be attained and more influence grown. This is a proactive and confident approach to our profession, which will drive better engagement through respect and willingness to represent a high level of craft quality and positive interaction.

Skill to Understand
Shared Decision Points

In order to have an understanding with your industry partners, you need to consider what their primary decision points are in the overall process. There are three design decision points that the contractor, developer, and architect share:

1 **Delivery of the project.** Safety, risk, and quality are the primary factors that define the successful delivery of the project. If the delivery of the project doesn't have the successful management of safety, risk, and quality, the project will fail, which will impact the following two decision points (profit and aesthetics).

2 **Profit from the project.** Equity, expense, and oxygen for growth (revenue) are the primary factors that define a profitable project. If a project is not profitable for that particular project type, then the project will fail financially and reduce the number of opportunities for future projects.

3 **Aesthetics of the project.** Beauty and an improved built environment are the primary factors that define the successful aesthetics of a project. People occupy buildings and places; they decide what to buy, what to rent, where to eat, and what type of atmosphere is the most satisfying to them. Their workspace may be inspiring, creating happiness and more productivity, or it may be unpleasant and uninspiring, creating the opposite reaction. Ignore the aesthetics and experience, and the project fails.

These three decision points are shared and are the common denominators unifying the contractor, developer, and architect. What will vary will be the priority of each decision point held by the contractor, developer, and architect.

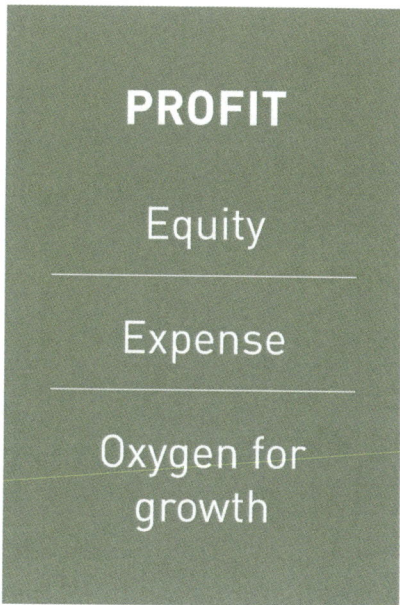

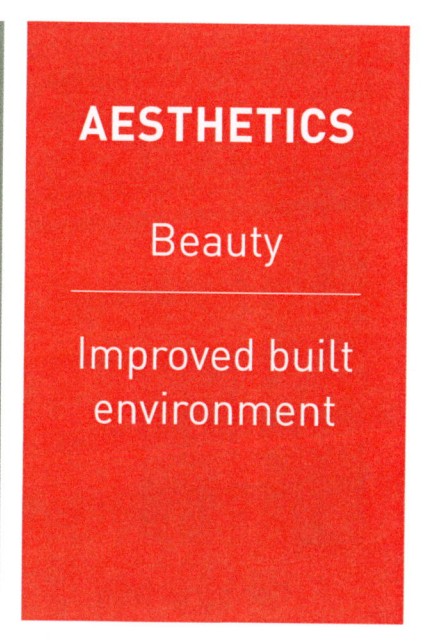

DELIVERY	PROFIT	AESTHETICS
Safety	Equity	Beauty
Risk	Expense	Improved built environment
Quality	Oxygen for growth	

Skill to Understand
Role-Adjusted Priorities

The driving factors within the primary decision points will vary and be adjusted based on the priorities of the contractor, developer, and architect. This creates role-adjusted priorities that will establish the overall partner priorities during a project. When these priorities are acknowledged by the architect, effective communication will increase with each group.

For example, when an architect is wondering why the contractor is not so concerned about an aesthetic improvement idea during the construction of the project, it is because the contractor is focused on the delivery of the project, which means that safety, risk, and quality are more important to them at that time. The architect needs to adjust their communication to align with the partner's priorities.

Construction — Delivery, Profit, Aesthetics

Development — Delivery, Profit, Aesthetics

Architecture — Delivery, Profit, Aesthetics

Skill to Understand
Trust Gaps

As the result of the role-adjusted priorities, trust gaps are created as they relate to the differences between the priorities. The gap represents the lowest of importance of a decision factor that defines a decision point.

For example, the lowest decision factors for the contractor during construction are additional aesthetic changes. The lowest decision factor for the developer is the delivery of the project; they rely on the contractor and architect to do their jobs for a successfully delivered project. The lowest decision factor for the architect during construction is profit; they are more worried about the design aesthetics being realized correctly, per the documents. If we recognize these trust gaps, it will help us to improve our craft skill in communication.

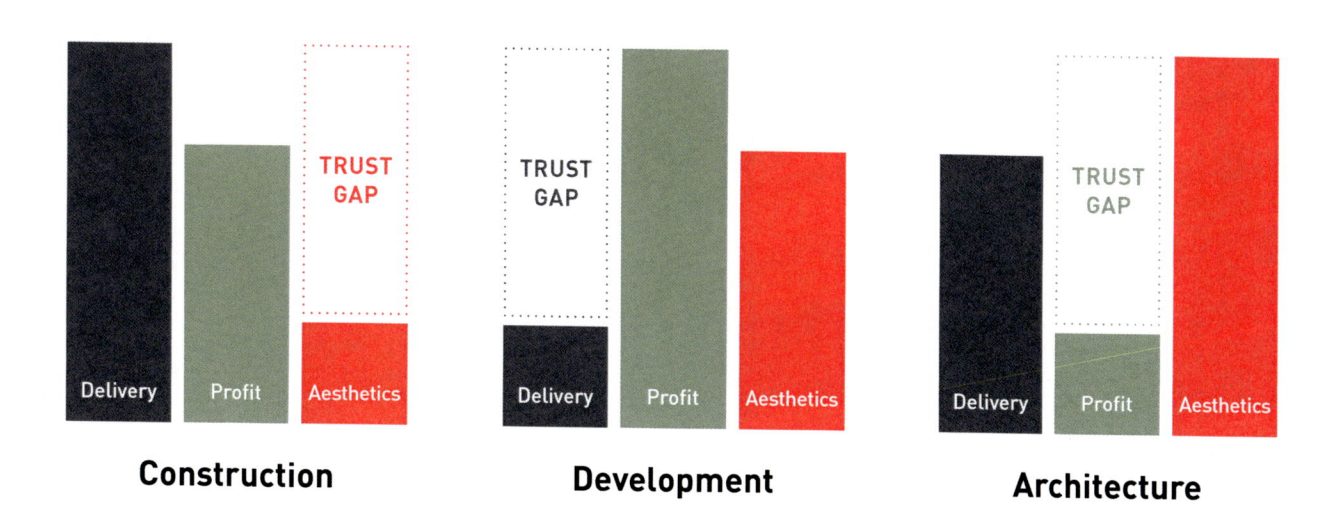

Construction — Delivery | Profit | Aesthetics (TRUST GAP)

Development — Delivery (TRUST GAP) | Profit | Aesthetics

Architecture — Delivery | Profit (TRUST GAP) | Aesthetics

THE CRAFT ADVANTAGE

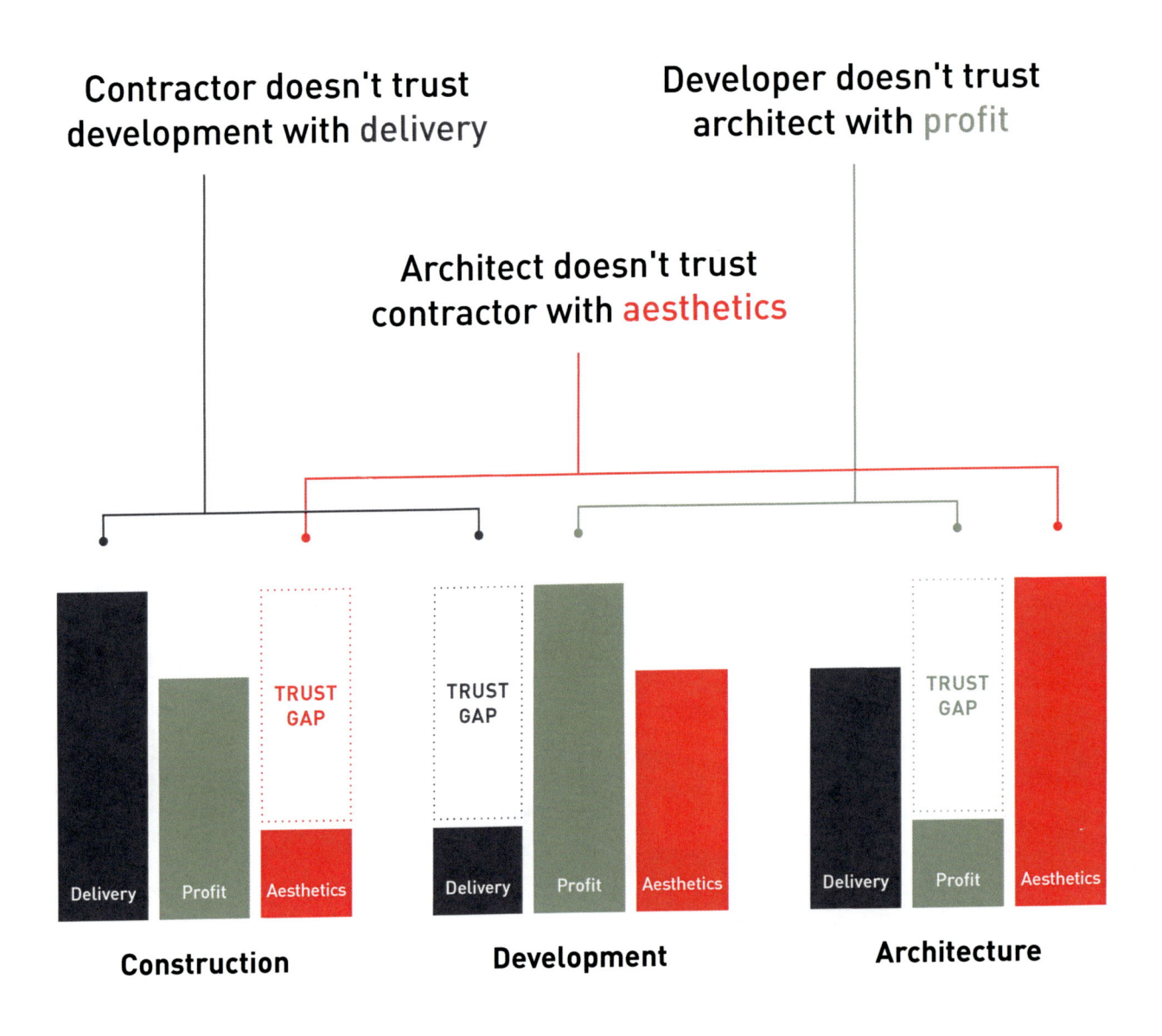

Contractor doesn't trust development with delivery

Architect doesn't trust contractor with aesthetics

Developer doesn't trust architect with profit

Construction	Development	Architecture
Delivery / Profit / TRUST GAP / Aesthetics	TRUST GAP / Delivery / Profit / Aesthetics	Delivery / TRUST GAP / Profit / Aesthetics

Skill to Understand
Long-Term, Shared-Priority Goal

The long-term, shared-priority goal is that we can build strong and trusted relationships with our partners so that each will trust their partner with their most important priority. This may fall into the category of "fantasy," but as I described earlier, I am a fan of reality and I am a delusional optimist. I think that it is possible as our partnerships and relationships mature and we each start to embrace the other's priorities. It is possible and a great long-term goal.

Just imagine what the relationships would be like if the contractor trusted the architect with the budget and the developer trusted the architect with the profit and the architect trusted the contractor with the aesthetics of a project.

It would be an amazing achievement that would increase profit, the number of project opportunities and relationships, and efficiency and create higher-quality projects and built environments. The architect's role in this goal is to revive craft as a core value once again to reverse the decline and grow our influence in the industry. Once we do this, the logical effect will be the contractor and developer aligning with our standard of craft and communication excellence.

Architects have been vision leaders throughout history. Being a vision leader is our natural role. When our confidence is high, as a profession, it is easy; when it is in decline and we are on the defensive, it is very hard to earn the respect needed to lead. Imagine the positive impact if we and our partners could earn the trust by respecting and supporting each other's roles, responsibility, and goals.

ARCHITECT		CONTRACTOR
Nonlinear	**F**	Linear
Less risk	**R**	High risk
Ideas first	**I**	Facts first
Optimistic	**C**	Pessimistic
Change world	**T**	Build project
	I	
	O	
	N	
	G	
	A	
	P	

Skill to Understand
The Friction Gap

In order to realize any long-term goal of being the vision leader for our industry, we need to focus on the short-term purpose of understanding our construction partners to facilitate a better working relationship with them. It starts with recognizing that we are different. We are educated differently, and we have different interests and priorities in our profession. We both have dominant tendencies that align with the role we each play. This may seem obvious to some, but it is useful to outline the differences for comparison:

1. **Nonlinear vs. linear.** Being nonlinear during the design can be a strength, but during construction, the contractor can't build a building in a nonlinear way, otherwise the building won't stand.

2. **Less risk vs. high risk.** This means that the contractor is closer to the reality of building the building and, therefore, has to take on more risk as a burden in turning the building into a reality.

3. **Ideas first vs. facts first.** This means that, during construction, the contractor is not interested in more ideas; rather, they are interested in the facts first that relate to building the building on time and safely.

ARCHITECT	CONTRACTOR
Nonlinear	Linear
Less risk	High risk
Ideas first	Facts first
Optimistic	Pessimistic
Change world	Build project

4. **Optimistic vs. pessimistic.** This doesn't mean that the contractor is not optimistic; it means that as the stakes get higher and as the building becomes real, the risk of failure is higher and they lean toward the answer of "no" for any new ideas that may burden the overall project budget and schedule.

5. **Change world vs. build project.** This means that the contractor is focused on the "now" of the project and not the future goals for a better world. It isn't that they don't care, but the "now" is their focus.

> These differences create the friction gap that can get in the way of effective communication. If we respect these differences, we will be more successful in communication with our construction partners.

Skill to Understand
Respecting Differences

Our mission to reduce the friction gap is to learn to respect our differences and varying priorities during each phase of the project.

During construction, the contractor takes on the dominant tendencies because they are the skills needed to manage their risk profile. But during the design phase, the contractor may be more open to new ideas and will, for the most part, embrace the architect's dominate tendencies.

Architects need to recognize that these dominant tendencies will shift depending on the phase of the project, and they should strive to bring up new ideas early in the process and not later when the contractor's risk profile increases and the dominant tendencies are more heightened.

Understanding these characteristics will motivate the architect to maintain quality while maintaining design speed to maximize opportunities for positive collaboration with construction. A slow design process will place more design decisions in the latter half of the project, and the friction gap will increase, making the project delivery and design quality more difficult to achieve. Moving with urgency is one of the best ways to help the contractor maintain their priorities. When you can help, you will build productive relationships that will help everyone during the project.

Skill to Understand
Value the Other's Priorities

The trick to reducing the friction gap and developing respect for the different tendencies of our industry partners during different phases of a project is to develop the skill to understand and truly value the other's priorities—not "pretend value," but actually valuing their responsibilities and pressures.

We need to realize that it is very hard to care about another's priorities when we are very busy caring about our own priorities. What is needed to make this easier is to set their priorities as one of your priorities. Make room on your list.

Consider their perspective and priorities as one of the design objectives of the project—because in reality, it is. You can't design and see a building realized to the highest level of quality without your construction partner. You need to do everything you can to align and understand the contractor's perspective so that you can maximize opportunities and quality on the project.

Keep in mind that when a project is successful, both the contractor and the architect look great to the owner. There is a great reduction of stress and an increase in joy at this point that turns into a deep appreciation for the team. This appreciation turns into future work and relationships that become more work and more relationships. Any time invested in valuing the other's priorities is never wasted.

Skill to Understand
Find the Joy

Why do what we do? What drives an architect to design and the contractor to build? It isn't because we love spreadsheets or schedules or design conflicts or value engineering or entitlement challenges or budget cuts or procurement delays or redesigns or the other many dramas associated with the designing and building of a project.

The act of realizing a building from nothing into something with people you barely know is an amazing and fulfilling endeavor. It is at the height of human interaction and achievement.

I have believed for many years that if the world were run by architects and contractors on a shared mission of realizing a better world, with a trust-centered collaboration culture as fuel, it would be a better place, for sure.

So, why do we do it? Answer: for the joy of it. It is truly joyous to realize a quality project. When the team finds the joy, they find a power of collaboration that can drive incredible quality. Our job as construction and architecture leaders is to remind the team of the joy of realizing a building as a team.

Find the joy, and you find the fuel for excellence in craft and an enduring influence.

Skill to Communicate
The Five Meetings

In your career, you will have many, many meetings. It is the nature of design communication, coordination, building relationships, damage control, and winning and losing work. In school, design is the priority, but what is not taught is that successful meetings are what provide the opportunity for design.

SCENARIO

You have been invited to a meeting for a new project opportunity for your practice. Pick the best path of action from the following options:

- (A) Arrive on time, listen intently, and take notes.
- (B) Ask for an agenda, arrive on time, and be prepared to ask questions.
- (C) Research where you can, be prepared, arrive early, and plan on staying a little later.

The best answer is C.

Arriving on time is good, of course, but arriving early is better and being able to stay late is better. Here is why: in my experience, there is an opportunity for five meetings for every one meeting to build relationships, gather information, and obtain a better understanding of your client and partners.

Meeting 1 is when you arrive early with other early attendees, gathering in the lobby or in the hallway and waiting for the conference room to be opened.

Meeting 2 is the "meeting" that involves waiting for those who arrive on time for the main event to enter the room. This meeting is for friendly conservation about the weather, holidays, weekend plans, sports, fun facts, and so on.

Meetings 1 and 2 are often very useful in understanding the true intent of the main-event meeting. This early information will help a person adjust to the context of the meeting. For example, maybe the meeting is the result of the owner or project manager being in trouble for starting the project late, or maybe you find out that the schedule will be the primary focus of the meeting. Any early information can help you be ready to engage most effectively. (Note: The "on-time" people have already missed two opportunities for more information.)

Meeting 3 is the primary meeting. Posturing, drama, action items, issue resolution, blame, forward motion, important information, money issues, schedule challenges, and new work are always possibilities in Meeting 3. Your main focus is to add value and increase your understanding.

Meeting 4 is when the main event, Meeting 3, is complete and people are lingering and chatting on the way out and into the hallway. This can be a happy or stressful exit, depending on the main event. If there was drama in this exit meeting, it is important that you don't add to it. If it was a happy meeting, continue the joy with friendly conversation as people exit to their next meeting.

Meeting 5 is in the lobby or parking lot or on the way to the car. This is often the most important meeting to learn information that may be less appropriate for a larger audience, to hear informally about new work coming down the path, to hear about leadership changes, and so on.

Best practice for Meeting 3: If it is in your office and/or the meeting is on a complex subject, bring a junior team member to take notes so that you can focus on the meeting to engage and contribute. The other consideration is that when you need to take your own notes, never let the note-taking be dominant. Aways have your eyes on the room, jot down a keyword only, and don't write sentences or paragraphs. Your primary mission is to give your full attention to the room and not to your notepad.

My process for Meeting 3: Listen and engage, jot down a note occasionally, add humor to the conversation, build off of sidebar conversations, propose solutions or recommendations, and be ready to help and accommodate needs. I have found that note-taking is a distraction, and I tend to remember better and understand the emotion of the room by intently listening, asking questions, and engaging with proactive dialogue. Keep in mind that some clients find it discomforting when the professional that they have hired is not occasionally writing something down. After the meeting, I may take a moment to send a summary email to my team or call to recap.

Meetings are a design activity of action and engagement. You can't make great design decisions without a great understanding of your client and their project needs. It is in meetings where you can learn the information to maximize project and client relationship success. Meetings take skill and practice to maximize value.

Final note: You are hired because you are an expert. You are hired to make life easier for your client and their team. You are not hired to come to a meeting only to ask questions. Why hire you if you don't have the answers? What would you think if your doctor asked you what you would like to do for treatment? When you ask questions, you can add stress to the client team. You are putting them on the spot. Instead, a best practice is to propose your solutions and recommendations and then ask for their input. Asking questions in reaction to their input creates a much more collaborative environment. Though you are an expert at integrating information into effective design, you are not an expert on how the client likes to operate, so always be humble and receptive to their input.

Always request a meeting with their facility team so that you can get information on the building maintenance, which can help you specify the correct material and design for the best solution that can increase operational ease. One thing to remember is that the facility people are there after you leave the project. You want them to say great things about your design and be your advocates.

PRIMARY SKILLS TO DEVELOP:

- Learn to remember instead of relying on note-taking. Have an active mind during a meeting, seeking opportunities to understand and contribute.
- Have an empathy filter to understand the issues and read in between the lines of any unspoken content.
- Learn to read a room. Be observant and thoughtful.
- When appropriate, follow up after a meeting with an email to document what was heard, issue meeting notes, and/or contribute to official notes sent out by the meeting owner.

Skill to Communicate
Meeting Types and Priorities

There are many types of meetings that will require a different level of preparedness, skill, and priority. Only through experience will you learn to recognize the differences. The more experienced reader will recognize the following types of meetings.

SCENARIO

Due to unexpected events, you are triple booked, and you need to decide which meeting to attend. Which of the following three meetings have the highest priority?

- (A) The project coordination meeting with the consultants
- (B) The project overview meeting with your team
- (C) The owner, architect, and contractor (OAC) meeting

The best answer is C.

The OAC meeting has the highest priority because it has the highest potential risk. Any meeting with the project owner is a high priority, but any meeting with both the owner and the contractor is the highest priority. The reason is that you want to make sure that your team is properly represented to the owner as design and construction issues are discussed. The OAC meeting is a report-out meeting regarding the status of a project under construction or in the design phase. This meeting can have many important challenges and issues that can cause some stress and need immediate leadership to keep confidence high with the owner and builder. If you are not there, design issues may be misinterpreted or presented as more problematic than they are, which can make the design team look bad and may impact winning future work. This meeting can be very political and require a sophisticated perspective and meeting skill to make sure that the relationships are effective and that the design team looks good at the end of the meeting.

Personal Presentation

Meetings may have different personal presentation requirements. Here are some guidelines:

1 **Formal.** Behavior and dialogue is at the highest and wardrobe is business casual or better, depending on the audience.

2 **Semiformal.** More casual in attire and professional dialogue.

3 **Informal.** Casual attire and less-guarded dialogue.

Major meeting "don'ts": No profanity, no yelling, no discussion of politics or religion, no personal attacks, no excessive editorializing, no inappropriate humor, and no putting down the competition or any other professional or client. The mission is to maintain the best professional image.

Meeting Types

1. **OAC meetings.** Semiformal; these meetings should have two people from the design team present.

2. **Internal coordination meetings.** Informal; these meetings happen, as required, to coordinate and develop project understanding.

3. **Client introduction meetings.** Formal, depending on your audience; always have business cards.

4. **Meetings on site.** Semiformal/casual; meetings on site often have project walks after the meeting, requiring personal protective equipment, boots, a hard hat, and so on.

5. **Client presentations.** Formal; these meetings happen to review the design progress.

6. **Interview presentations.** Formal; these meetings occur often after being short-listed to interview, require rehearsal and practice, and can determine if you win or lose a project.

PRIMARY SKILLS TO DEVELOP:

- Be prepared and learn to determine the priorities and mission of a meeting.

Skill to Win
The Next Project

The hardest activity is winning the next project. Each project represents "oxygen" for your team. The oxygen is revenue to keep growing. Revenue follows projects. With this in mind, it is necessary to develop the skills to win work over time. Each pursuit is different and will have its own unique constraints, so there is no set way to win work, but there are some fundamentals and techniques that are often useful in the search for new work. You should be aware that you will lose more pursuits than you will win ... Be ready, and stay optimistic. It is important to never give up.

SCENARIO

Your team is active for the next six months. After six months, you are looking at a revenue cliff and need new work to keep your revenue at the correct level to support your team. What should you do?

(A) Cut back on expenses to save money and conserve your cash flow to survive the cliff.

(B) Ask your current clients if they have new work planned in the near future.

(C) Research project boards for upcoming Requests for Proposals (RFPs) and Requests for Qualifications (RFQs).

(D) Connect with your consultants and construction partners on upcoming work and design-build opportunities.

The best answers are B, C, and D. Answer A may be necessary, but it is a last resort because it can have side effects that can reduce your chances of getting new work, such as a lower team morale; reduced marketing efforts; and reduced external activities, such as conferences or community volunteering.

Finding new opportunities and winning new work are the results of building relationships over time and staying connected to the community. I believe that there are four primary categories:

1. **Repeat work with existing clients.** This can be facility work to help ongoing operations of an existing campus and/or facility or helping to set the table for future growth through master planning services that can lead to new projects.

2. **Responding to RFPs and RFQs.** Companies and public entities will advertise RFPs and RFQs for their project team needs. The distinction between the two is that an RFP is requesting a cost for a certain service and an RFQ is requesting qualifications before discussing costs for a project need. (Note: Public work, depending on the city and state, will disqualify an application if cost is included in an RFQ.)

3. **Random opportunities.** These are project opportunities that appear unexpectedly through relationships, community engagement, existing industry partnerships, and being in the right place at the right time. The key to this category is to be always listening and paying attention to your surroundings.

4. **Created opportunities.** This is my favorite category, but it takes the most time to realize a project. It is based on horizon seeking for your clients and requires creativity, vision, integrity, intellect, research, and providing free work to help your clients prepare for the future. The effort may not produce a project in the end, but it will build relationships that may result in more work later. [Two very important notes: 1. Too much free work will diminish your value and revenue. Use very good judgment on when free work is appropriate. 2. Don't help with the expectation of getting anything in return. Help because you care about your client or future client. If you can't do this, don't engage in this category.]

PRIMARY SKILLS TO DEVELOP:

- Learn to see beyond. Practice horizon seeking (Intelligent Idea Integration).
- Provide support without obligation. Recognize that a little help can make life easier.
- Be aware of your surroundings. Keep an active mind with attentive hearing.
- Never give up. Start early to build a backlog.

Skill to Lose
Lose to Your Advantage

You will lose more opportunities than you will win. Losing work is common and always painful. Because it is common, you need to develop skills to turn the negative into a positive.

SCENARIO

You were short-listed for a project interview and are competing with five other teams. You were just notified that your team lost the interview. What should you do?

(A) Meet with your team to determine where the weakness was in the team presentation.

(B) Move onto the next opportunity.

(C) Request a meeting with the owner to discuss the scoring and where you could have done better.

(D) Protest the decision.

The best answer is C (first). This option provides the following: (1) it provides information to improve or understand the overall context; (2) it shows the client that you value their input, your desire to improve, and you are not sensitive to criticism; and (3) it opens the door for learning more about the client, a possible future relationship, and follow-ups for future work. It is during this type of meeting that you get insight into future work opportunities, sometimes, as a consolation.

When a team does their very best, you will know it. The interview will harmonize and feel great. Losing doesn't mean that the team did badly. The reality is that winning work is only based, in part, on qualifications. The other ingredients are internal politics, external politics, and chemistry. You have no control over these factors.

Options A and B are good but only after C. Option D is rarely a good option.

Option A is a great way to brainstorm improvement and build your team relationships by celebrating the good and having "eyes wide open" on any areas of improvement. When this is performed as a team, the team gets tighter.

Option B is obvious: take what you have learned and apply it to the next opportunity.

Option D is not recommended, but at times, it is necessary in the architecture world. I shy away from the idea of protesting, but protests are an option when you think that there has been something significant that has been overlooked or compromised to your deficit (for example, if the allotted interview time was cut short; if it was stated that "no leave-behind information packets" were allowed, and you noticed that a team provided them to the reviewers; or your interview time had only some of the reviewers, as some had to leave early for another meeting). If you can determine an unfair playing field, then you can notify the purchasing agent who is responsible for the interview process. It is very delicate work to protest with grace.

PRIMARY SKILLS TO DEVELOP:

- See the opportunities in loss.
- Have a candid dialogue with the team, potential client, and purchasing agent.
- Follow through on improvements.

Skill to Grow
Recruit and Retain

You are only as good as your team. No project is realized by one person, no matter how brilliant and creative they are. Your team is everything, and that means that you need to recruit the very best that will fit your team culture, firm goals, and skill needs.

SCENARIO

You have a new project coming up ahead of schedule that requires two more people than you currently have on your team. You need to hire. How should you proceed?

- (A) Put an ad in the paper with the American Institute of Architects (AIA), on LinkedIn, or on Craigslist.
- (B) Go to your "warm bench" to activate people who are interested in joining your team.
- (C) Ask other professionals.

The best answer is B.

This is tricky because hiring begins with finding someone who can fit the role and your team culture, being able to pay for a new hire, and your timing of need. These are very hard to align. If you have an immediate need and you do not have a warm bench, then you will be forced to accept someone who may not fit the culture. In the short term, you may have accommodated the project need, but in the long term, you may find yourself dealing with internal chemistry challenges and conflict issues between other team members. This takes valuable time and can create distractions that can affect the productivity, joy, and harmony of the team. Recruiting before your need arises is the key to stable and effective team building.

Establishing a warm bench is not a perfect science, to say the least. It is the result of finding like-minded people who are currently working elsewhere but may have an interest in joining your team in the future. The key to the warm-bench approach is ensuring that they are currently employed and that, in the future, you can offer them a growth opportunity, which means more money and more career growth. If you can't, then it is less likely that they would want to make a move.

Additional ways to improve warm-bench opportunities are volunteering and teaching undergraduate and graduate students who can be interns in your practice. They may not have a great deal of architecture knowledge, but they are very good at software, graphic presentations, diagramming, rendering, researching, Revit/AutoCAD, and learning fast.

Recruitment requires vision for the right types of team members and the ability to convey your vision for the team and their opportunities. If you can't communicate a vision for your practice, you will have a difficult time recruiting top talent.

Skill to Adjust
Deficient Design

Stating the obvious, we are all human. Your team will make errors. You will make errors, and your trusted partners will make errors. It is life. It is also life that some will not handle it well and focus on the negative, deflect, and find a target to blame.

> "Fix the problem, not the blame" is great advice.

Though an error may have been innocent, the result of incompetence, or random, it doesn't really matter. It can have a significant impact on your reputation and your client's perception of your team, potentially reducing the opportunity for future work. It could also result in lawsuits or arbitration.

I have been fortunate enough to have never experienced lawsuits and/or arbitration, but it doesn't take experience to know that it is a painful process that may have been avoided if there was not an error.

Damage control is the art of navigating these waters with the least amount of damage to your firm, team, and relationships.

SCENARIO

You discover during construction that a design solution in your construction document (CD) package is not aligned with best practices, and while not being unsafe, it could result in a less-than-satisfactory product for your client. Exposing the deficit to the client and contractor would be embarrassing. What should you do?

- (A) Because it is not unsafe, keep quiet to protect your reputation and chance for future work.

- (B) Meet with the contractor to seek a solution that can be presented in unison to the client.

- (C) Request a meeting with the client to expose the issue and ask them what they would like to do.

The best answer is B.

Architects have an impact on the built environment and people's experiences for many years. Poor design solutions may be forgotten by the architect over time, but the client will suffer the errors for years to come. When an architect discovers a design deficit, they are obligated to resolve it to the best of their ability, even if it means a hurt reputation. I believe that doing the right thing is the best option, regardless of possible negative blowback. In time, the right thing proves to be the best option.

Answer B is the best course of action because the contractor usually has the same goals as you do: a happy client, a desire to do the right thing, an interest in a high level of craft, and reducing possible warranty claims. If you see a problem, engage the contractor as soon as possible with solution options for their review and input. Be willing to accept compromise and alternate ideas where they make sense. Remember that, in most cases, your solution is not in the budget that the builder is working with, so the fix has to be cost-effective. If you are united with the builder, they may be able to use contingency dollars for the fix. If not, then you will need to ask the client, unified with contractor, to authorize additional contingency funds for the project (the client, in most cases, will have their own contingency). This is an uncomfortable situation, but what makes it tolerable is that you are united with the builder and you are doing what is right. In the end, most clients appreciate the care for quality even though they may not like the unexpected increase in cost.

Answer A is unacceptable for the reasons already mentioned, and **Answer C** is very bad because you are transferring stress and responsibility to the owner when you should be taking ownership of the issue.

PRIMARY SKILLS TO DEVELOP:

- Seek creative solutions to difficult discoveries.
- Have candid, intelligent, fearless conversations and follow through to achieve the best for your client.

Skill to Deliver
DBB, CMaR, or DB

When you can, try to pick or influence the delivery-method decision with the owner. Think of the delivery method as the road map or recipe for the whole project through post-occupancy. If you use the wrong map, you may find yourself lost, and if you have the wrong recipe, the meal may not taste great. The following is a high-level summary of key distinctions to consider when deciding which method will be the best for your team and the project. Oftentimes, you will not have a choice, but having an idea of the distinctions will help you manage outcomes.

1. **Design-bid-build (DBB): More time, high-quality documents, and less collaboration.** This is the traditional delivery method that has been used with great success over many years and is actively used today. The process is in the title. The architect designs and creates the "instructions" to build the project. The design documents go the market of contractors to get a bid on what it will cost to build the project. Then, based on their bid and qualifications, the constructor is selected for the project.

   Key advantages: This process requires that the drawings are the most detailed and well coordinated to ensure the most accurate price.

   Key disadvantages: This process requires more time, and the architect and contractor don't have a collaborative relationship during the design to help to build the project. This often results in more conflicts, more change orders due to the competitive bid process, and an unpleasant experience for all involved.

2 **Construction Manager at Risk (CMaR): Less time, average-quality documents, and more collaboration.** This delivery method started to appear to accommodate the need for speed to market and the best value for the client by reducing change orders to the project that were often seen in the DBB process. The idea is that if the contractor and architect can be contracted separately and start basically at the same time, they can collaborate during the design process to have reduced changes during construction so that the client will get the best value for their project.

   Key advantages: This process is faster, involves fewer change orders during construction, and is often more fun.

   Key disadvantages: This process involves average-quality drawings due to moving fast and its tendency to rely on field coordination/collaboration during the design process to put less detail into the drawings. This shifts more risk into the construction phase, which is remedied with the construction contingency but often makes the architect lose money during construction administration (CA). The contractor plans for the refinements and expense, and the architect often doesn't, losing money and getting less detail quality realized.

3. **Design-build (DB): Less time, lower-quality documents, less collaboration, and more directed decisions.** DB can be very effective, depending on the quality of the construction team. If they respect the roles and responsibilities of the design professionals, then it can be an amazing experience. If they don't, it is horrible for the architect, and the client receives a lower-quality design.

   Key advantages: This process is very fast and cost-efficient.

   Key disadvantages: This process involves lower-quality documents, an often lower-quality design for the client, and more design decisions directed by the contractor due to expediency (and not directed by the best design decision for the overall project). DB can often create average-quality aesthetics.

Pick wisely when you can. If DB is the selected method, make sure that the team supports transparency and the roles and responsibilities of the design professionals.

Skill to Breathe
Profit, Loss, Resource Planning, and the "Cliff"

It is a common fact in architecture that the architect often loses money during CDs and CA. The fee is often mismanaged during the early phases of the project based on a focus to get the design right, not necessarily to get it done efficiently. "Getting it done right" is an excuse for a lack of discipline or a lack of trying to be better at making great decisions quickly. It isn't about money; it is about time and discipline—discipline in process to keep moving forward and discipline in thinking to nail down the ideas quickly. Front-end speed and effectiveness may come down to talent and experience, but I think that they can also be learned skills with practice.

Profit is oxygen to keep breathing. There is no escape from this fact in our profession. When the fee is spent due to an ineffective process, it slowly removes oxygen from the practice. Without oxygen, there is no growth. Everything we do in practice should be geared toward increasing oxygen by winning more work and refining and respecting the process to use the available oxygen most efficiently.

The following are high level and simplistic steps to consider:

1. **Calculate your project fee** with a built-in profit of 20% for each billable hour. Calculate your total fee to have a 20% contingency. This is my 20-20 rule. It is not perfect and will need to be adjusted to get a competitive fee balance, but overall, it is a good place to start.

2. **Calculate how much you can lose**, which is the full fee minus the 20-20. Take the difference and convert it to hours. This is your hour cushion to breakeven as the result of inefficiency and unexpected internal challenges. (Note: This cushion is not for new client scope. New scope is an added fee). For example, if this calculation equals four weeks and the full fee with 20-20 is twelve weeks, then I know that if I hit the twelve weeks with the same staff, then I have made my 20-20 profit. If I missed the schedule by four weeks, then I have broken even.

3. **Resource planning.** Now that you have created a fee and know the schedule and the number of people on the project, you need to make sure that you have the right people at the right time so that the project is delivered based on your cost model. If you have only one project, this is easy. But when you have multiple projects, it is very complicated and never perfect.

4. **The "cliff."** Compare your resource planning across all of the ongoing projects and then overlay any future projects. This activity will do two things: (1) reveal when you have too much staff or too little staff at a particular phase of work and (2) reveal when you will have a "cliff." The "cliff" is the projected time that you will run out of work (oxygen) for your team.

> **If you don't find more oxygen to keep breathing, you will need to reduce the size of your team or other areas of expense.**

Skill To See
Slippery Role Syndrome (SRS)

There are unique personalities that I have encountered that can have a negative impact on the quality of a meeting and the project experience. I created the acronym SRS to describe this adverse behavior, with the hope that, when you experience it, you can be prepared for the annoying and sometimes destructive interaction and deter any future SRS behavior in another team member. Slippery role syndrome (SRS) is when a person "slips off" their role to assume another person's role within the meeting.

SCENARIO

You are in a weekly OAC meeting during the construction phase of a project. In attendance are twenty team members representing the design, construction, and ownership. While the project schedule is being discussed, the client asks the contractor how many weeks the schedule will be affected by this design decision. Who should answer the question?

(A) The construction project manager

(B) Anyone other than the construction project manager

If you chose Answer B, then you may be afflicted with SRS. Answer A is correct because the schedule question was directed to the construction project manager. Respecting roles is critical for a happy, high performing team.

This is a characteristic that I believe originates from a team member's insecurity with their responsibility and possibly their position in their career. They can't help but speak their opinion even though the question is not directed at them and the content of the question falls outside of their role and responsibility. They should stay quiet and let the person who is responsible for the content address the question.

When you encounter this kind of behavior on your team, I recommend the following:

- After the meeting, advise them one-on-one of the adverse behavior that you have witnessed and the potential impacts to the team when roles are not respected.

- If they can't or won't stop the behavior, then remove them from the meeting. Do not fear offending them. Team unity and effective interaction are more important than one person's feelings and their lack of desire to make changes for their own skill improvement.

Project delivery is very complicated for both small and large projects, but when a project is large, the potential negative impacts increase when roles are not respected and communication is hindered by SRS. Oftentimes, the larger the project, the larger the team that will be present in the weekly meetings. The more people there are, the higher the potential for communication gaps and unproductive sidetracks.

> **SRS wastes time and reduces the positive flow of a project.**

Skill to See
Build, Then Coordinate, Then Blame (BCB) Syndrome

Another unique personality or deficiency that I have encountered with some contractors is what I have labeled BCB. I have created this acronym to describe this adverse behavior with the hope that if you experience this pattern you can stop it early before problems occur and the relationship with construction and the owner are irretrievably damaged.

Build, then Coordinate, then Blame (BCB) syndrome is when a contractor, due to inexperience, poor training, and/or just a disrespectful construction culture, ignores the architect's drawings and their responsibility to coordinate before starting to build. They decide to build the project without doing a full confirmation of what they are building. After realizing that their lack of 'coordination before building' has resulted in problems they shift blame to others, like: the architect, subcontractors, the owners, the owner's representatives, and users.

The BCB syndrome either originates from a poorly trained construction partner who is feeling scheduling pressures to move quickly and who doesn't want to concern themselves with the appropriate process, or it comes from their leader telling them not to worry about the architect, just the schedule. BCB is more likely to be seen when working with a bad design-build contractor.

SCENARIO

You are on a design-build project, and you visit the job site for a field inspection and find out that an aspect of the building has been built incorrectly and is contrary to the design and the reviewed submittal. You also find out that the builder has ignored these issues and other coordination items related to the deficiency that are important to the overall project. What should you do?

- (A) Meet with contractor to determine why they didn't follow the submittal review process.
- (B) Advise the owner that the contractor is not following the process to ensure that the design is being built per the CDs.
- (C) Going forward, unless there is an acknowledgment of the oversight in process and changes are made, mark all relevant submittals "revised and resubmit" to force the resolution.

The answer is A, first, then C, and then B. This situation is complex. First, you are in a design-build relationship with the builder, which most likely means that you are contracted to the builder. Second, your contract with the builder doesn't remove you from your professional and ethical responsibilities to ensure that the design that you have put your professional seal onto is being built correctly, per the approved design documents. Third, you want to maintain a good relationship with the builder to keep the process enjoyable and effective for the team and owner.

Answer A: Meet and discuss the process, and hopefully the failure was an oversight that will not be repeated. If so, move on with no further action. If not, then choose Answer C.

Answer C: If you don't get an appropriate response from the builder and you have confidence that the adverse pattern will continue, then I recommend that all following submittals be marked "revise and resubmit." The reason is this: In a design-build relationship, you don't have much power, and you depend on an environment of mutual respect for roles and responsibilities. If that mutual respect is not there, then the process is flawed. Rejecting the submittal can cause the contractor great concern because it shifts risk onto them. They want their architect to review and approve the submittal for their own risk management. When the architect rejects the submittal, their risk increases, and it forces the contractor to either own all the risk or change their process and behavior. This is the best chance to make change happen. The owner benefits when the contractor and architect are aligned.

Answer B is the worst case. If the building is being built without following the approved documents and the builder refuses to change their behavior, you need to advise the owner and plan on never working with that builder again unless their process and manners improve.

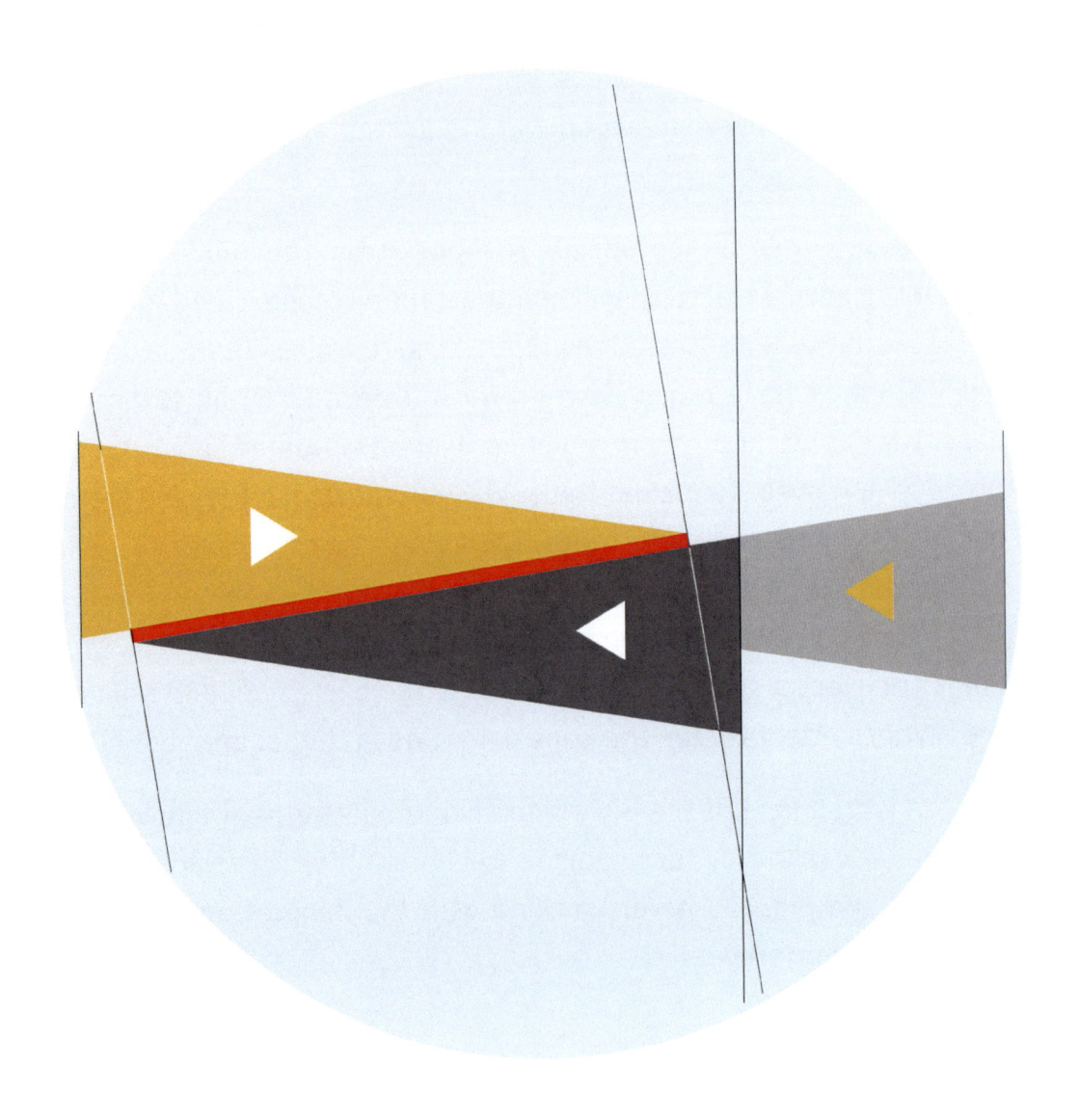

The Super-Architect: The Future of Architecture

Skill to Integrate
The Super-Architect

I will be describing the future of architecture, AI integration, our relationship with construction and what it means to be a Super-Architect. The following is one example from the upcoming book outlining the next level relationship with construction for growing our future influence in our profession. In this section, I have included a summary of the goals, characteristics, and processes required to take our relationship with the construction team to the next level to achieve design excellence, combined with construction excellence, to advance the goal of the Craft Advantage for greater quality and influence over time. The Super-Architect includes the superintendent and the architect as the leaders for the design integration of the project and project delivery. A Super-Architect is a team made up of the superintendent and the project architect, who have an integrated partnership from the beginning and until the end of the project to maximize quality for the client and lead an optimal partnership between the architecture and construction team. In order for this high-performance diagram to become real, the following traditional team organization has to be changed.

Typical Construction Team Organization

The construction project manager is in charge of the project, including the money, schedule, and delivery. The superintendent reports to the project manager. The project manager reports to the project executive. The superintendent is in charge of managing the construction on site. This traditional format emphasizes project money management skills over experience in building a building.

Typical Architecture Team Organization

The architect project manager is in charge of the project, including the money, schedule, and delivery. The project architect reports to the project manager. The project manager reports to the project executive. The project architect is in charge of the CDs. This traditional format emphasizes project money management skills over project design integration skills, drawing integration and detail expertise. Both the construction and architecture management format disconnect the superintendent and the senior architect from working together, hand in hand, from day one because of cost, staff scheduling and predictable control. In the Super-Architect diagram, they start working directly together from the beginning until certificate of occupancy and beyond, if needed

The Super-Architect Team Organization

The project managers for the architect and construction teams stay in charge of the money and schedule but not the design integration or project delivery. Because the superintendent and the project architect decisions are the closest to the reality of realizing the design and the successful construction of the project, they need to have fewer layers and filters in their decision-making process and more responsibility to lead. This diagram requires the architect project manager and the senior architect to be a team reporting to each other and reporting as a team to their project executive and, then, connecting through perforated siloes to the same team diagram on the construction side. This will result in better team integration placing the skill and talent closer to the need.

SKILLS TO SHAPE

The Super-Architect team starts the project together at the beginning and works hand in hand throughout the project to ensure maximum integration between the design, design documentation, and construction practice. At the end, the client can have the very best project with the fewest unexpected changes. It will also increase talent retention and growth for both the construction and architecture firms by allowing the roles to be aligned with the most effective realization of and responsibilities for a project. When this team alignment is fully embraced and practiced, it will result in superior design and construction integration. As a result, both the architect and the construction teams will see lower profit erosion and less cost impact to the client.

Project architects will get better by working at the beginning with the superintendent. The superintendent will get better by working early with the project architect. Both learn what the other knows for better growth. My Super-Architect diagram will maximize quality and be an amazing step toward realizing better teams, a better built environment, and the Craft Advantage. This new format will challenge the many existing and 'structural' preconceived organizational expectations that each team will have, but, if the idea can be realized it will represent the next level relationship between the architect and the builder and an opportunity to further advance the architect's influence. More to follow in next book as it relates to Super-Architect benefits, risks, possibilities, contracts, detailed work planning, design innovation, sustainability advancement and process.

"Courage is the first of human qualities because it is the quality which guarantees the others."

ARISTOTLE

CONCLUSION

We are in a very tough profession. It is easy to feel beaten down while trying to maintain the goals of others, your goals, and your team's goals and trying to achieve quality, over and over again. It is tough to build relationships that are lasting. It is very difficult to find work, to win work, and to realize the best quality project possible. We start out in school with big goals, we enter the profession with our values intact, and the industry proceeds to try and squash away our values—if we let it.

We need to have the courage to maintain our values for craft, design excellence, and an improved built environment. We need to keep our vision of a better world through an engaged architecture profession. We are about the vision. We are trained to think about the future, and we need to live up to that challenge. The best way to do this is to strive to be excellent at what we do, to be experts in our specialties, and hold a high standard in craft that is unmatched in our industry. High craft skill will push back attempts to compromise quality. When we are unified in values, the quality is higher, the fees are higher, the influence is greater, and, ultimately, our positive impact is greater. We become essential beyond a doubt and the leaders for craft excellence in our industry. We are not just sitting at the big table; we own it.

The Craft Advantage is my recommendation to become unified, once again, around the core value of craft to maximize our influence for a powerful profession and a beautiful and better built world. Our effective future depends on care and craft maximized.

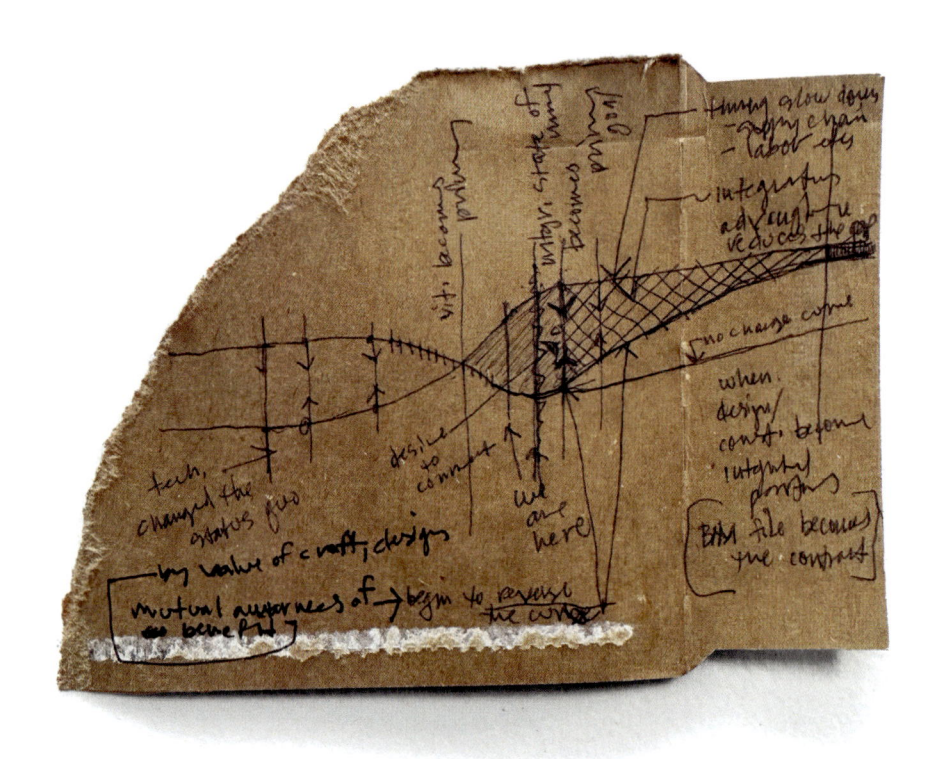

The sketch that inspired this book

THE CRAFT ADVANTAGE

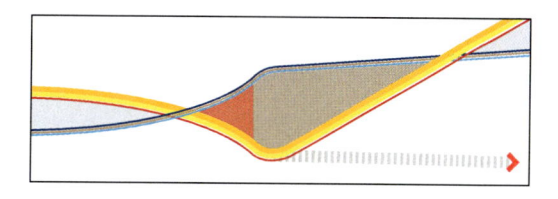

WIDEN YOUR GAZE

BEAU DROMIACK is an award-winning architect who began his architecture career as a junior in high school working for a two-person architecture firm, drafting and building models. When the office work was slow, he would be sent into the field to help construct the houses he had helped to craft. His first design-build project was an outdoor amphitheater's concrete podium for his high school. He worked his way through college drafting, drawing perspectives, creating renderings, and making models while working for small architecture practices needing support. After graduate school, Beau began his professional career working in a cabinet shop and for a well-known artist/architect. It was during this time that Beau learned a deep appreciation for craft. It was also during these formative years that he left the primary pursuit of unique architectural expression to develop a deeper understanding of what drives reduced quality in the overall built environment and the complex profession of architecture.

As a result, Beau sought out various professional experiences, ranging from small artist/architect firms to corporate architecture firms and engineering-dominant architectural/engineering (A/E) firms to establishing and leading a national design-build company's first southwest regional A/E team. He has extensive integrated design expertise.

Now Beau is pursuing way more architecture as principal of a newly revived firm in Phoenix, Arizona, focused on advanced, mission-critical integrated design projects.

Beau has developed a broad expertise in design-bid-build, CMaR, design-build, and integrated design delivery. He is a member of AIA, DBIA, SCUP, and NCARB. He has a master of architecture degree from Arizona State University and teaches as an undergraduate and graduate student professor and mentor. He volunteers teaching design to design-build teams at the Northern Arizona University School of Construction. He is an active volunteer, teaching STEM-focused architecture and engineering principles to elementary school students, and has developed STEM teaching tools to expand the student understanding of architecture and engineering. Beau has been married for thirty-three years and has four adult kids: one son and three daughters. He loves backpacking and nurturing chickens to achieve the best egg. He is also an avid cookie baker, pursuing the best cookie experience. He is a very active hobbyist and loves coffee, thoughtful conversation, reading, analog vinyl, and fly fishing.

Beau's mission is understanding the future of architecture and a better built environment through expanded experiences and the transfer of profound and often hard-earned wisdom to like-minded professionals seeking a better built environment and profession.

Made in the USA
Middletown, DE
01 February 2024